THE
LITTLE
BOOK
OF
SCOTLAND

GEOFF HOLDER

To Glastonbury Coromandel

First published 2014
Reprinted 2016

The History Press
The Mill, Brimscombe Port
Stroud, Gloucestershire, GL5 2QG
www.thehistorypress.co.uk

British Library Cataloguing in Publication Data.
A catalogue record for this book is available from the British Library.

ISBN 978 0 7524 9332 9

Typesetting and origination by The History Press
Printed in Turkey by Imak.

CONTENTS

ILLUSTRATIONS

The illustrations are taken from the following publications:

A History of Scotland for Schools by P. Hume Brown (1907)
An Account of the Bell Rock Light-House by Robert Stevenson (1824)
Boy's Own Annual (1905)
Chatterbox (1914)
The History of Scotland by James Mackenzie (1894)
The Humorist (1923)
Larousse Petit Encyclopédie Illustrée (1906)
London Opinion (1920)
The National Burns (1879)
Punch (1882–1919)
Sir Walter Scott by W.S. Crockett & J. L. Caw (1903)

As ever, many thanks to Ségolène Dupuy.

INTRODUCTION

Oh, ye'll take the high road,
and I'll take the low road,
And I'll be in Scotland afore ye.

You probably know these lines – they're from the famous traditional Scottish song 'The Bonnie Banks o' Loch Lomond'. So well known is the song that it gave its name to *Take the High Road*, a Scottish daytime soap opera that ran from 1980 to 2003. The series was filmed on Loch Lomond – the very place celebrated in the song's lyrics: 'For me and my true love will never meet again, On the bonnie, bonnie banks of Loch Lomond.'

Nobody really knows how old the song is, nor what the lyrics mean. The song has usually been interpreted as a lament related to one of the Jacobite rebellions. Other people think it may have something to do with a criminal due to hang in England, or perhaps a tale of the supernatural – is the 'low road' the land of the dead? All these interpretations, however, may be wide of the mark. Quite simply, this beautiful, emotional and universally known ballad is a complete mystery.

That, to me, sums up Scotland. A country of worldwide fame, with a distinctive culture and a strong heart, it is nevertheless something of an enigma.

Some parts of Scotland's story are universally celebrated or championed, while other aspects have been neglected, even obscured. It is widely perceived as a romantic land of castles and mountains, and yet the vast majority of its people live in modern cities. A simplistic view of continual tension with its southern neighbour clouds a much more complex history of shifting allegiances and enmities within Scotland itself, often reflected in the fundamental geographical and cultural difference between the Highlands and the Lowlands. Even the elements that commonly define Scottish identity – the kilt, the bagpipes, tartan – have changed their meaning so much that a visitor from, say, just two centuries ago, would struggle to understand how it is they mean so much to modern Scots.

And so here you will find many surprising, hidden and quirky aspects of Scotland, from history to hovercrafts, from whisky to wine, and from extreme food (haggis, anyone?) to some extremely odd sports.

Welcome to a Scotland that is strange, marvellous, madcap, dark, glorious, peculiar, and spectacular – often all at the same time.

Take the high road.

1

PLACES –
HERE & NOW,
THEN & THERE

PREHISTORIC DAYS

The oldest calendar in the world was constructed by nomadic hunter-gatherers in Aberdeenshire 10,000 years ago. Twelve wooden posts set up at Warren Field near Crathes Castle mimicked the phases of the moon and recorded the lunar months, allowing the seasons to be followed. The Mesolithic device is almost 5,000 years older than the first recognised formal calendars known from ancient Mesopotamia.

Aberdeenshire contains approximately 10 per cent of all the 900 stone circles in Britain.

The Ring of Brodgar on the mainland of Orkney is the third largest stone circle in the world. The numerous prehistoric monuments in the area are collectively listed as a World Heritage Site known as the Heart of Neolithic Orkney.

Callanish on Lewis in the Western Isles is one of the most elaborate prehistoric sites in Britain. Featuring a stone circle with a cross-shaped series of stone rows, the complex is focused on the 18.6-year cycle of the moon across the heavens.

Lewis also has the tallest standing stone in Scotland. The Clach an Trushal monolith is over 19ft in height.

One of the most spectacular prehistoric sites is at Machrie Moor on Arran, where seven stone circles stand in close proximity to each other.

A prehistoric monument unique to Scotland is the broch, a cylindrical stone defensive/residential proto-castle that looks like a scaled-down power station cooling tower. Double-skinned, the walls were honeycombed with internal stairs and chambers. Brochs survive to a reasonable height in Lochalsh, Skye and the Western Isles. The best is at Mousa in Shetland.

The mysterious stone monuments of the Neolithic and Bronze Ages were still regarded with awe into the modern age. Many burial mounds were thought to be the home of fairies or spirits. Women visited various stones thought to promote conception and/or a safe childbirth at Darvel (East Ayrshire), Pitreavie (Fife), Dingwall (Ross & Cromarty, Highland) and Clach-na-bhan (Aberdeenshire). Such visits continued until at least the mid-nineteenth century.

WHAT DID THE ROMANS EVER DO FOR US?

Hadrian's Wall did not mark the limit of the Roman Empire. There are two (far less well-known) Roman frontiers further up Scotland: the Antonine Wall (AD 142–144), parts of which can still be seen on the narrow neck of land between Glasgow and the River Forth; and the Gask Ridge, a true 'Wild West' frontier of forts and watchtowers

running from Camelon in Falkirk District north-east through Stirling District and Perth & Kinross to Stracathro in Angus.

Having been built between AD 70 and AD 80, forty-two years before the start of building works on Hadrian's Wall, the Gask Ridge is the earliest fortified land frontier in the Roman Empire. It effectively separated the fertile plains and important harbours of the Lowlands from the less valuable (and more difficult to control) Highlands – perhaps the first political recognition of the fact that Scotland has two distinct geographies. The tensions and differences between the Highlands and the Lowlands have remained a factor of Scottish life ever since.

In the first century AD the Roman army briefly penetrated even further north, reaching Aberdeenshire, Moray and as far as present-day Inverness.

The idea that everyone in Iron Age Scotland painted themselves with blue woad, lived a wild but free life and hated the Romans is

a myth that has its roots in misguided nineteenth-century romantic patriotism. Some Lowland Caledonian tribes were more than happy to take bribes of silver and luxury Mediterranean goods (like wine) in exchange for not disturbing the *Pax Romana*. And a number of Lowland farmers did very nicely selling grain and other agricultural products to the hungry Roman troops. Even Hadrian's Wall wasn't the military exclusion barrier it has been portrayed as – many of its gates were open most of the time to allow the passage of goods and animals for market – goods and animals, that is, sold by the local tribes.

Roman influence in Scotland ebbed and flowed, depending largely on what was happening elsewhere in the Empire. After AD 211, with a few exceptions, the Romans largely withdrew to Hadrian's Wall.

In 1772 the pioneering traveller Thomas Pennant was given a Roman coin which had been found on the shore at Greshinish on Skye. The Romans never reached the area, leaving us to wonder how a denarius bearing the image of the Emperor Trajan (AD 98–117) reached this remote spot.

The belief that an entire Roman legion was annihilated in AD 117 somewhere in Scotland has inspired a number of works of fiction, notably Rosemary Sutcliff's 1954 novel *The Eagle of the Ninth* and the films *The Last Legion* (2007), *Centurion* (2010) and *The Eagle* (2011). The story, however, is nothing more than a modern myth: the supposedly vanished Ninth Legion was still in existence after the alleged Scottish battle, and it disappears from the records only after a later, unknown, conflict in the eastern part of the Roman Empire.

WHAT'S IN A NAME?

You would think the name Scotland means 'the land of the Scots', the Scots of course being the indigenous people of the country that lies north of England. Nothing, however, is ever that simple.

To the Romans, the area north of Hadrian's Wall was called Caledonia, and at least some of the people who lived there in later times were known as the Picts. The Scots, meanwhile, were actually a tribe from Ireland, the Dal Riàta, who didn't arrive until the sixth century, long after the Romans left. Initially the Gaelic-speaking Scots only controlled the western seaboard of their new country, while most people still called the place Pictland. Had they not won their

generations-long conflict with their Pictish neighbours, the Scots may
well have disappeared from history and the national anthem would
today be 'Pictland the Brave'.

But never mind the Scots coming from Ireland; Dark Age Scotland
was nothing like the Scotland of our times. The south-west was part
of the Kingdom of Strathclyde, stretching from north-west England
as far as Glasgow, and home to a Brythonic (Celtic British) people
who spoke Old Welsh. The south-east – including Edinburgh – was
meanwhile occupied by the Angles of Bernicia (whose Anglo-Saxon
language became the basis for the modern Scots variant of English).
And the Northern and Western Isles were the stamping ground of the

Vikings, who introduced numerous Norse-speaking settlements. With various ethnic peoples speaking Welsh, proto-English, Gaelic, Pictish or Norse, the idea of 'Scotland' as a unitary nation in the seventh and eighth centuries was ludicrous.

The Scots eventually became the dominant people in much of the central part of the country, creating a kingdom known as Alba. Pictish as a language and a cultural identity disappeared, replaced by the Gaelic culture and language of the new overlords. Over time, Alba of the Scots became referred to as Scotia, and by the early eleventh century there was finally a country which almost everybody called Scotland.

CASTLES

Conflict creates castles. If there are men with sharp pointy things coming to kill you, then it makes sense to defend yourself in the best way possible. There are records of perhaps 2,000 castles in Scotland, of which around 1,200 still exist today. Some 'castles' are really nineteenth-century luxury houses with twiddly bits, while others are the full-on medieval real deal.

The most common Scottish castle is not the vast, hugely expensive royal fortress such as those found at Edinburgh or Stirling, but the family stronghold, a relatively modest tower house designed to protect a small number of kinsmen from marauders.

Castles first make their appearance in the eleventh century, with the earliest stone-built castles dating from about 1200. This means that Macbeth (king from 1040 to 1057), for example, would have never walked a stone battlement or entered a great hall made from anything other than earth and wood. Filmmakers, take note.

The most visited castle in Scotland is Edinburgh Castle, which receives more than 1.3 million visitors a year.

Even if a castle is in ruins, there is usually one feature that survives: the garderobe, or toilet, which typically projects outward from the wall – and is often placed directly above the moat. You can imagine the consequences.

The most northerly castle is the sixteenth-century Muness Castle on the island of Unst in Shetland. Like most Scottish castles, it is modest in size, and its history is stained with blood.

Castles, of course, attract legends. When visiting ruined Duntulm Castle on Skye, for example, you might be told that the castle was abandoned because a nursemaid accidentally dropped the heir to the MacDonald chiefdom onto the jagged rocks below. You might even be informed that the window where the accident took place still exists, and that any young woman who looks through it will be cursed with a barren womb. Before swallowing this story hook, line and sinker, it might be worth knowing that exactly the same story is told of at least six other castles throughout Scotland.

Scottish castles are also famous for being haunted, and guides tend to get a bit fed up of being asked, 'Where are the ghosts?' Whisper it quietly, but some castles have been known to keep visitors happy by inventing the odd ghost or two …

THE MARCH OF TIME – LOST COUNTIES

There are three certainties in life: death, taxes, and changes to local government boundaries. In Scotland, the many variations inflicted on the various county councils mean that names that were once part of the landscape and culture are now largely lost, and what used to be one place is now an entirely different place – which is confusing if you're trying to find the modern map location for somewhere mentioned in family history research, a historic document, or a Walter Scott novel.

To be fair, the situation before the reforms of 1890 was at times baffling and bizarre. There were thirty-four counties, some of which, curiously, had 'offshoots' in other counties, leading to all kinds of administrative craziness when it came to registering births and deaths, or paying taxes. The northern county of Cromartyshire, for example, was actually nine separate enclaves entirely surrounded (and separated) by the much larger Ross-shire. Nairnshire had colonies in both Inverness-shire and Ross-shire. Lewis was governed by distant Ross-shire, while Harris – part of the same island – was the responsibility of Inverness-shire. In the Borders, a tiny part of Selkirkshire nestled inside neighbouring Roxburghshire. And in the heartland, Clackmannanshire cut both Perthshire and Stirlingshire into two parts each, while Stirlingshire itself sliced Dumbartonshire in half. It was, frankly, a right pig's ear of a system.

The situation after 1890 became a little more sensible, but there were still some name changes to come. Haddingtonshire became East Lothian, while Linlithgowshire transformed into West Lothian. Forfarshire was now Angus, and Dumbartonshire changed one letter to become Dunbartonshire. Zetland, meanwhile, became Shetland.

In 1975 the thirty-three former county councils were reorganised into just twelve regions: Borders, Central, Dumfries & Galloway, Fife, Grampian, Highland, Lothian, Orkney, Shetland, Strathclyde, Tayside and the Western Isles. Some of the regions were ungainly, clumsy creations – Strathclyde Region, for example, stretched from the metropolis of Glasgow to the remote islands of Coll and Tiree, whose combined population would barely fill a Partick tenement. In 1996, when the regions were abolished in the most recent shake-up, Strathclyde Region was broken up into no less than twelve councils.

Although the regions were little loved as administrative units, their names (and catchment areas) are retained in official bodies such as Strathclyde Partnership for Transport or Tayside Fire & Rescue.

Several counties disappeared in the 1996 reforms. In the south-west, the names Dumfriesshire, Kirkcudbrightshire and Wigtownshire vanished, as did the Borders counties of Peebles-shire, Selkirkshire,

Berwickshire and Roxburghshire, plus Nairnshire in the north. Banffshire and Kincardineshire became subsumed in greater Aberdeenshire. A large part of Perthshire was shifted into Stirling District, and then Perthshire was married to Kinross-shire to become Perth & Kinross. In practice, most people still use the original names – even the tourist board prefers 'Perthshire' to 'Perth & Kinross'.

There are currently thirty-three council areas in Scotland, and these are the ones referred to when indicating locations in this book.

In the south and south-west:

Dumfries & Galloway	South Ayrshire
Scottish Borders	East Ayrshire
North Ayrshire	South Lanarkshire

In the Central Belt (the most populous area):

Inverclyde	North Lanarkshire
Renfrewshire	Falkirk District
West Dunbartonshire	West Lothian
East Dunbartonshire	City of Edinburgh
City of Glasgow	Midlothian
East Renfrewshire	East Lothian

In the Heartland:

Clackmannanshire	Perth & Kinross
Stirling District	City of Dundee
Fife	Angus

In the north-east:

Aberdeenshire	Moray
City of Aberdeen	

And in the north and west:

Argyll & Bute	Orkney Islands
The Western Isles	Shetland Islands
Highland	

The smallest county on the mainland is Clackmannanshire, where around 50,000 people live in just 60 square miles: hence the nickname, 'the Wee County'. The largest county by far is the Highland Council area – which is bigger than four of the next largest counties put together – so often a subsidiary, more usefully local name is appended, such as Caithness, Sutherland, Wester Ross, Cromarty, Skye, Lochalsh or Strathspey.

Just to muddle matters further, the administrative county known as 'Highland' does not include all of the geographical area known as 'the Highlands'. So you can be in the Highlands but not be in Highland. Yes, it's confusing – but that's local government for you.

I suspect that more local government changes of name and boundary await us in the future.

THE MARCH OF TIME – CHANGING FORTUNES

It wasn't until 1437 that Edinburgh became the capital. In fact, the city was not even in Scotland at all until the year 1020.

The Borders county of Berwickshire disappeared in the administrative shake-up of 1996. But it had lost its county town long before. After a great deal of to-ing and fro-ing in the wars with England, Berwick-upon-Tweed had been finally taken by the English in 1482, and to this day remains just south of the border. In 1596 the much smaller Greenlaw was designated as the new county town of Berwickshire. In 1661 the nearby town of Duns snatched the title. As being the county town had all kinds of advantages, not least financial, Greenlaw took it back in 1696. Duns and Greenlaw then argued about the matter for hundreds of years, and it was not until 1903 that Greenlaw finally lost its status as county town.

PLACE NAME PECULIARITIES

The longest place name in Scotland is the eighteen-letter Coignafeuinternich, which is an abandoned village in the Monadhliath Mountains west of Aviemore (Highland). The name is Gaelic, a language which cleaves to long words. Norse, in contrast, tends to be terse, and gives us the shortest village name in Scotland – Ae in Dumfries & Galloway – as well as uninhabited places like Aa and Ve (Shetland) and Oa (Islay).

You can have a Brawl in Caithness (Highland), meet Mavis Grind in Shetland, and walk through Muck (Inner Hebrides). Take care, however, when dealing with Hen Poo (Scottish Borders), Rotten Bottom (Dumfries & Galloway) or Tongue of Gangsta (Orkney).

The village of Dull in Perth & Kinross is paired with the Oregon town of Boring.

If you are in Aberdeenshire you could get some Blankets, call someone Fattiehead or Tarty, watch out for your Backside in case of Brokenwind – and then get Lost.

Other names to please or vex the tongue are Maggieknockater (Moray), Brainjohn, Easter Auquhorthies and Yondertown of Knock (Aberdeenshire), Slackend (West Lothian) and Puddledub (Fife).

With Zetland becoming Shetland in 1890, there are now only two places in Scotland beginning with the letter 'Z', and they're both called Zoar: one is in Forfar in Angus, and the other is a farmstead west of Hillswick on Shetland.

There are no places in Scotland beginning with X.

Balfron in Stirling District is occasionally visited by Star Wars fans seeking a connection with the fictional planet of the same name.

Should you wish to go overseas without leaving Scotland, you could head for New Orleans in Argyll or Moscow in East Ayrshire.

Beware pronunciation: Milngavie in Glasgow is pronounced 'Mulguy'; Findochty in Moray is 'Finechty'; Friockheim in Angus is 'Free-come'; Strathaven in South Lanarkshire is 'Straven'; Garioch in Aberdeenshire gets warped into 'Geerie'; Footdee in Aberdeen is 'Fittie'; Hawick (Scottish Borders) becomes the throat-clearing 'Hoyck'; Wemyss in Fife is 'Weems,' while nearby Kirkcaldy is rendered as 'Kir-cawdie'; and Kirkcudbright in Dumfries & Galloway trips off the tongue as 'Kir-coo-brie'. Why? Just because.

The abandoned coastal village of Fishtown of Usan in Angus was once known as Ulysseshaven.

Deep inside the Cairngorm range is a mountain called The Devil's Point. The original Gaelic name, however, is Bod an Deamhain, or 'The Penis of the Demon'. According to Cameron McNeish's 1998 book *The Munros: Scotland's Highest Mountains*, the name was changed when Queen Victoria asked what the mountain was called. Her guide, the famous John Brown, was too embarrassed to use the real translation, and so the euphemism has remained as the English name ever since.

Close to Campbeltown in Argyll is a small mountain some 617ft high. Its official name is The Bastard, although no one seems to know why it is thus called.

The northern half of the Aberdeenshire village of St Combs was once known by the name of Sodom – and the inhabitants were hence referred to as Sodomites.

SCOTLANDS AROUND THE WORLD

For centuries Scots have left their native land as soldiers of fortune, as political or religious refugees, as prisoners, economic migrants, forced labourers, and as the unwilling victims of the Highland Clearances. As a consequence, the number of places around the world named after a location in Scotland, or a Scottish person, is so great that the list would fill an entire book. Here are just a few examples.

In the United States, there are Scotlands in Connecticut, Georgia, Indiana, Maryland, Ohio, South Dakota and Virginia. In New York state, New Scotland is joined by Scotchtown, Scotchhill, Scotch Church and, slightly bizarrely, Scotch Bush. A Scotland County can be found in each of the states of Missouri, Maryland and North Carolina. Maryland also has Scotland Beach and Scots Fancy, while Iowa gives us Scots Grove and Scotch Glen. Scotlandville is part of Baton Rouge in Louisiana. North Carolina has its Scottish Hills and Nashville its Scottish Highlands, while Scotland Run is in New Jersey, which also claims Scotch Plains and the slightly unusual Scotch Bonnet.

To give one example of Scottish influence in America, take the case of the state of Pennsylvania. As well as possessing a Scotland, a Scotch Hill, a Scotch Valley and a Scotch Hollow, Pennsylvania has approximately 580 other places named after Scottish locations or people. In fact, every one of the state's sixty-seven counties has at least one place name of Scottish origin.

As well as naming part of the American continent, Scots may have been among the very first Europeans in the New World. According to the 'Saga of Thorfinn Karlsefne', an Icelandic saga first written down in the thirteenth century, Thorfinn, who headed the second Viking expedition to America around 1007, had with him two fast-running Scottish slaves named (in Norse) Haki and Hekja. Thorfinn put

them ashore first, largely as bait. After three days the slaves had not been attacked by any natives, so the Vikings deemed it safe to come ashore and camp. The saga, sadly, makes no further mention of what happened to Haki and Hekja.

There are three New Scotlands in Canada, two of them being in the province of Ontario, and the third in the Maritime province of New Brunswick. Nova Scotia (Latin for 'New Scotland') is another of Canada's east coast Maritime provinces.

British Colombia, Canada's westernmost province, was originally called New Caledonia. Caledonia was the Roman name for Scotland, and gained popularity with Scottish writers and poets in the nineteenth century (Sir Walter Scott famously coined the phrase 'O Caledonia! stern and wild').

Caledonia was the name of the doomed colony established by the Scots in Panama in the 1690s. The 'Darien Disaster', as it came to be known, almost ruined the Scottish economy.

New Caledonia, a large tropical island in the Pacific with a population of around 250,000, is a territory of France (the official name is Nouvelle-Calédonie).

Johannesburg in South Africa has the world's largest cluster of suburbs named after Scottish locations, with twenty-four names across some 6 miles of city, including Morningside, Glen Atholl, Heriotdale, Birnam and Balmoral.

New Zealand and Australia both have major concentrations of Scottish place names, and the river in the former's city of Dunedin – Gaelic for Edinburgh – is even named after the Scottish capital's Water of Leith.

Within the Antarctic Circle you can find the South Orkney Islands and the South Shetland Islands, while the Falkland Islands are, via the Viscount of Falkland, named after the palace in Fife. Antarctica also has a Dundee Island and its own Firth of Tay.

These days 'Scotland Yard' is synonymous with London's Metropolitan Police. The Met's original nineteenth-century headquarters had its public entrance on a street called Great Scotland Yard, which may have got its name when diplomats from still-independent Scotland lived there in the sixteenth and seventeenth centuries.

The Pacific island nation of Vanuatu was once known as the New Hebrides. Hong Kong has Aberdeen Harbour, Java hosts Glenmore, and you can find Macduff, Iona and Glasgow in Sri Lanka. There's a Bannockburn in Zimbabwe, a Glencoe in Trinidad and, in Jamaica, Culloden.

There are in fact hundreds of Scottish place names scattered across Jamaica, and many Jamaicans bear Scottish surnames such as Campbell, Douglas, Farquharson, Ferguson, Frazer, Gordon, Graham, Grant, Lamont, Lewis, McDonald, McFarlane, McKenzie, Reid, Robinson, Russell, Scott and Stewart. Both place names and personal names are the legacy of Scotland's massive involvement in the slave trade. In 1800 some 300,000 slaves on the island were administered by a handful of Englishmen – and 10,000 Scots, for whom Jamaica was the place to make their fortune. Many Scottish slave masters became millionaires. Slave-grown sugar and tobacco powered the eighteenth-century Scottish economy and led directly to the growth of Glasgow, Greenock and other cities.

SCOTLAND IN SPACE

Six craters on Mars are named after Scottish places – Ayr (Scottish location: South Ayrshire); Balvicar (Argyll & Bute); Banff and Echt (both in Aberdeenshire); Darvel (East Ayrshire); and Doon (a loch and river in South Ayrshire).

The Dorsa Geikie, a tectonic ridge system on the moon, is named after Edinburgh-born Sir Archibald Geikie, one of the pioneers of nineteenth-century geology. In 1882 Aberdonian astronomer Sir David Gill took the first successful photograph of a comet. Gill Crater on the moon and its namesake on Mars are named after him.

When Neil Armstrong took his 'one small step for man, one giant leap for mankind' in 1969, and became the first human being to walk on the moon, he was carrying with him a tiny scrap of Armstrong tartan.

Two asteroids in the asteroid belt have craters with Scottish place names: 253 Mathilde is home to Clackmannan Crater, while 243 Ida boasts Fingal Crater, named after Fingal's Cave on the isle of Staffa.

Europa, one of the larger of Jupiter's sixty-seven moons, has a linear feature named after the prehistoric stone rows at Tormsdale in Caithness, plus a 'large ring feature' caused by the impact of a meteorite or other space debris, which takes its name, appropriately, from the amazing stone circle of Callanish in the Western Isles. Europa also has a region of 'chaotic terrain' which has been given the fantastic, science fiction-sounding name of 'the Arran Chaos'.

NAE LIMITS

Many people – including VisitScotland – claim that the most northerly place on mainland Britain is the small village of John O'Groats. This is not true. Dunnet Head, 11 miles to the north-west, is a little over 2 miles further north, and there are several small populated places with a latitude above John O'Groats – the northernmost settlement on the mainland is actually the tiny hamlet of Scarfskerry.

The actual claim to fame for John O'Groats is that it is one end of the longest distance between two inhabited points on mainland Britain (the other being Land's End in Cornwall).

The southernmost point in Scotland is the Mull of Galloway, which is further south than Carlisle in England.

Falkirk's Tolbooth Street used to hold the title of the shortest street in Britain, although its crown has recently been usurped by Ebenezer Place in Wick (Caithness/Highland), which is all of 6ft 9ins long. To qualify as a street a thoroughfare needs to have a doorway opening out onto it.

The highest pub in Scotland is not in the Highlands but in the Southern Uplands of Dumfries & Galloway. Wanlockhead, home to the Wanlockhead Inn, is Scotland's highest village, standing at 1,531ft above sea level.

The most remote pub in mainland Britain, however, can be found in Inverie, in Knoydart (Lochaber/Highland). The Old Forge can only be reached by ferry from Mallaig, or by walking over the hills from Loch Hourn to the north. Tiny Kinloch Hourn, at the head of Loch Hourn, may be the loneliest mainland settlement connected by a public road: the winding, steep and little-used single-track road from Glen Garry runs for 22 miles of emptiness, with not a single building for the last 12 miles. This must be one of the most spectacular car journeys in Britain.

In 1943 the Ordnance Survey commenced the process of resurveying and remapping the whole of Britain. The last place to be mapped was Durisdeer in Dumfries & Galloway, where a completion ceremony took place on 25 May 1982 – thirty-nine years after the project started.

ISLANDS

There are 790 islands in Scotland, of which 130 are inhabited.

Only about 2 per cent of the islands are found on the east coast. The major groups are the Shetland and Orkney Islands to the north, and to the west, the Outer Hebrides, the Inner Hebrides and the islands in and beyond the Firth of Clyde.

In line with recent renamings of places around the world, the Outer Hebrides are now officially referred to (far less evocatively) as the Western Isles, possibly because the original name suggested an unwelcome remoteness. In practice, both names are used.

The largest Scottish island is in the Western Isles – the combined island of Lewis and Harris.

The most northerly island – and hence the most northerly point in the UK – is Out Stack, just off the larger Shetlandic island of Unst. If travelling directly north from Out Stack, the next stop is the North Pole.

Skaw on Unst is the most northerly settlement in the UK. Bruray, on the Out Skerries archipelago (Shetland), is Britain's most easterly settlement. The sea-girt islet of Rockall, far to the west of the Western Islands, is the most westerly point of the UK.

Rockall is actually disputed territory. Ireland, Denmark and Iceland all claim that it belongs to them.

The islands of Shetland and Orkney only became part of the Kingdom of Scotland in 1471. Formerly belonging to Norway, the Scandinavian influence on the islands remains strong.

Lerwick, the capital of Shetland, is over 300 miles from Edinburgh. By contrast, Bergen in Norway is only 230 miles away.

The Isle of Man was part of Scotland from 1266 until 1334.

In the Middle Ages, the kings of Scotland, being bound to the mainland, always had great difficulty with their cantankerous subjects in the distant Hebrides. It took centuries before the 'Lords of the Isles' finally acknowledged the authority of the Edinburgh-based monarchy.

The Black Isle in Ross & Cromarty (Highland) is not an island. Neither is the Isle of Whithorn in Dumfries & Galloway.

The fantastically named Gulf of Corryvreckan, between the islands of Jura and Scarba, is home to the third-largest whirlpool in the world.

There are seven islands in the Slate Island group of the Inner Hebrides, but there used to be eight. The slate quarry on Eilean-a-beithich was hollowed out to well below sea level – and in 1881 the sea breached the quarry wall. Now the only sign that there was once an island here is the outer rim of the flooded quarry, looking for all the world like a miniature caldera of a sea-swamped volcano.

Sometime before the First World War, the Royal Navy decided to use the rock of An t-Iasgair (off Skye) for a bit of target practice, reducing its size by probably around 30 per cent.

You won't find Viking-Bergen Island on any maps, but it once lay between Shetland and Norway before the sea level rose around 6,200 BC.

At low tide you can walk from the Scottish mainland to no less than seventeen tidal islands, including Cramond Island near Edinburgh, Eilean Tioram (with its castle) in Loch Moidart, and Brough of Birsay in Orkney. Make sure you return before the tide does.

In Robert Louis Stevenson's classic adventure story *Kidnapped*, David Balfour, the hero, believes himself to be marooned on the Isle of Erraid. He spends four desperate days there before realising the island is tidal, and he could have walked across to the Isle of Mull whenever the water was low.

Ailsa Craig, south of Arran, was sometimes referred to as Paddy's Milestone, as it was a familiar marker for emigrants on the ships coming from Ireland.

Innis Eabhra was an enchanted island that supposedly appeared occasionally off the coast of Arran. It was last reported in 1864.

HOLY ISLANDS

The profusion of islands on the west coast formed part of the 'sea highway' that existed between Scotland and Ireland in the Dark and Middle Ages. From language and trade to religion and culture, the Irish influence on these islands has been profound.

St Columba came from Ireland in the sixth century to found the great abbey on Iona. From this tiny island, Christianity reached out across pagan Dark Age Scotland. Iona remains a place of pilgrimage for many people from different flavours of Christianity.

Many Scottish islands such as Iona, Oronsay, Eileach an Naoimh and Egilsay have provided a sanctuary for saints, hermits and monasteries. The Holy Isle, in the lee of Arran, once the home of a Christian hermit, is currently owned by a Buddhist community. Buddhist prayer flags and paintings make for pleasant surprises in the typical Scottish landscape.

ISLAND LIFE

The most populous island is the Mainland of Shetland, where around 17,500 people live with some of the strongest winds in Europe.

Thirty-one Scottish islands have fewer than twenty inhabitants.

Shuna in the Slate Islands has a resident population of three, while six islands have just two people living on them.

When the writer-intellectuals Samuel Johnson and James Boswell undertook their famous 'Tour to the Hebrides' in 1773, most people on the mainland (not just in England but in Lowland Scotland as well) knew more about the tribes of remote Pacific archipelagos than they did about the people of the Hebrides.

In 1715, Sir Donald MacDonald of the Isles set off the fight for the Jacobites. Fearing the consequences for his property should he be on the losing side, he cautiously buried the title deeds to the MacDonald estates on the almost unclimbable Am Bord ('The Table'), a rock off the coast of Skye. The island therefore has the alternative name of Lord MacDonald's Table.

In the early 1950s the residents of Bernera, off the coast of Lewis, were so desperate for a road link that they threatened to dynamite the cliffs and build their own causeway. The authorities gave in, and in 1953 a bridge crossed the 200-yard gap between Bernera and Lewis.

Since the construction of the Skye Bridge in 1995, the Isle of Skye could now technically be regarded as part of the mainland. No one, however, takes this idea seriously.

After almost ten years of protests, non-payment, arrests, prosecutions and further protests, the hugely unpopular tolls charged on the Skye Bridge were dropped, and the crossing is now free.

Some 3 million Spanish gold doubloons are reputed to lie somewhere in the waters off the Isle of Mull. Mull is also one of the most popular islands with tourists. This is probably just a coincidence.

By their very nature, islands make excellent prisons. Bass Rock in the Firth of Forth was used for political prisoners for over 200 years. Mary, Queen of Scots was a captive on Castle Island in Loch Leven (her castle prison is still there; it is possible to visit by boat from Kinross). French prisoners of war were held in the island castle of Threave (Dumfries & Galloway). And the unfortunate Lady Grange, wife of an Edinburgh Jacobite conspirator, was secretly hidden on the remote island of Heiskar off North Uist, and then for several years on St Kilda, the most isolated community in the British Isles, where no one spoke English. By the time Lady Grange was brought to Skye many years later, she had lost her mind and was in no position to reveal her husband's plots.

St Kilda is 41 miles west of the nearest landfall, Benbecula in the Western Isles. In the eighteenth century just one boat a year would call, carrying the factor, who collected rents. In 1876 the starving St Kildans contacted the outside world in the only way possible – by putting a letter in a sealed wooden container attached to an inflated sheep's bladder as a float. The cry for help reached Scotland and these tide-born 'mailboats' became the standard way to communicate with the mainland.

The islanders of St Kilda were evacuated in 1930 at their own request, as they could no longer feed themselves. The deserted island is now a World Heritage Site and a key destination for a small number of hardy visitors each year. Even today the minimum journey time by sea is eight hours – and that's if the weather isn't too rough.

MOUNTAINS

Perhaps more than any other physical feature, Scotland excites the imagination with its mountains. The Cuillin on Skye, the Seven Sisters at Glen Coe, the dramatic Torridon Hills in Wester Ross – these are defining images of what people around the world think when they refer to Scotland.

The majority of the highest mountains are in the north and the west, although the less well-known and lower Southern Uplands in the Scottish Borders and Dumfries & Galloway can offer walks and sights the equal of the Highlands.

The Highlands can be more or less defined by the Highland Boundary Fault, a geological fault line that crosses Scotland diagonally from the south-west to the north-east. Generally, the land to the north and west of the fault is topographically distinct from the lower land to the south and east. One of the places the difference can be seen is at Loch Lomond: the extreme south of the loch is a relatively gentle Lowland landscape which contrasts with the rougher, higher land as you move north up the loch.

Because of Scotland's high northern latitude, even a modest increase in altitude has a profound effect on both the natural world and human activities. In the mountains, there is less arable land, the soil is less fertile, the growing season is shorter, and it's harder to get around. All this means that life in the Highlands has historically been very different to that in the relatively more benign Lowlands.

The great cultural struggle in Scottish history is not – as is usually portrayed – between Scotland and England; it is between Lowland and Highland.

All mountains in Scotland with a height above 3,000ft are named Munros, after Sir Hugh Munro, the mountaineer who first listed them in 1891.

'Munro-baggers' can spend a lifetime seeking out and climbing the 282 Scottish Munros. The first known person to have ascended all the Munros is writer and mountaineer Hamish Brown. Since his achievement in 1974, over 4,000 people have followed in his footsteps.

Hills with a relative height of at least 150m or 492ft – that is, the distance between the summit and the nearest low ground, rather than absolute height above sea level – are called Marilyns. Yes, it's a pun – Marilyn Munro, you see.

The highest mountain in Scotland (and in Britain) is Ben Nevis, near Fort William (Highland). Around 110,000 people a year slog up to the summit.

By world or even European standards, Scottish mountains are small scale. But this does not mean they are easy. Atrocious and unpredictable weather is common and can be fatal. Around twenty people die every year whilst walking or climbing in the Highlands, many of them experienced mountaineers.

Heading into the mountains without adequate preparation puts not just your life at risk, but also those who turn out in all conditions to rescue you. In 2011 there were 573 accidents on the Scottish mountains, an increase of 22 per cent from 2001. The incidents required 24,000 hours of effort by mountain rescue teams, all of whom are volunteers.

The plateaux of the Cairngorms range often attain genuine Arctic conditions, with bone-chilling wind and extensive snow.

The Cairngorm Mountain Rescue Team is the busiest in the country.

2

SCOTTISH PEOPLE

Scotland has about 70 per cent of the landmass of England, but with only around 10 per cent of the population of its southern neighbour. The Scottish population is expected to top 5.3 million soon.

90 per cent of the Scottish population lives in the Lowlands, mostly in cities and large towns.

WELCOME TO THE DARK AGES

The period between the Romans finally quitting Britain (AD 410) and the rise of the medieval Kingdom of Scotland is one of the most fascinating (and least understood) periods of history, largely because there are so few documents that survive from an era of endemic warfare, invasion and disease.

Anyone who reached their mid-30s in Dark Age Scotland was considered old: the average lifespan was between 26 and 29 years. It was probably what is called a 'high fertility/high mortality' society, where women gave frequent birth as soon as they reached the menarche, although few of their children would reach adulthood.

Dark Age Scotland had no currency (partly because there was no single central authority that had the power or the means to issue coins). The elite tended to demonstrate their wealth by wearing massive and very heavy chains of silver around their necks – barbarian bling.

Slavery was widespread; the slave markets were filled with captured enemies, or simply people taken in coastal raids. Around AD 403

St Patrick, the future patron saint of Ireland, was sold as a slave, having been abducted by Irish pirates from his home in south-west Scotland (or Cumbria, or Wales – the sources are not clear).

To get an idea of domestic life in the Dark Ages, visit the reconstructed house at Bostagh on Bernera in the Western Isles. The structure on which it was based dates to some point after AD 500 and was uncovered by a storm in 1993. Sitting inside the dark, smoky, thatched building on a stormy day is a powerfully atmospheric experience. Remarkably, the house's format is not all that different from the 'blackhouses' that were the standard farmhouse design on Lewis until the late nineteenth century – a continuity of 1,500 years.

No examples of writing in Pictish are known, but the Picts contributed the most enduring artistic legacy of Dark Age Scotland – the Pictish Stones. These highly decorated stone monuments display exquisite carvings, including warriors, animals and battle scenes. Some of the symbols, however, are so abstract and so enigmatic that even today scholars can't agree on what they really mean.

The National Museum of Scotland in Edinburgh has a superb collection of some of the best Pictish stones, but others are scattered up and down the country, often in ones and twos, and seeking them out in their obscure locations is a highly recommended way of exploring Scotland off the beaten track. Particularly good examples can be found in Meigle (Perth & Kinross), Aberlemno (Angus) and the Highland sites at Inverness, Rosemarkie, Portmahomack, Nigg and Dunrobin.

No less than four chronicles written by monks between 891 and 906 state that a woman cast up on the shore somewhere in Scotland had several distinguishing features:
Skin: 'all white as swan's down'
Hair: 17ft long
Height: 195ft
Was this a female giant, taller than any building standing in Britain at the time? What was this really? Some kind of whale? Or a giant squid? We'll never know.

WHAT DID THE VIKINGS EVER DO FOR US?

Although a small number of Scandinavian colonists had set up shop in Shetland as early as the seventh century, the Viking era properly

started with hit-and-run raids in the year 793. Many of the early targets were unprotected religious establishments such as the Abbey of Iona (sacked in 802 and 806). In recent years there has been some attempt to downplay the 'murder, rape and pillage' image of Viking plundering, but a reading of the chronicles makes it clear just how brutally ferocious these raids were.

Raiding soon gave way to full-scale colonisation, or, to put it another way, invasion. Shetland, Orkney, the Western Isles, the Inner Hebrides, the islands in the Firth of Clyde, Caithness, Sutherland, parts of Argyll – all became Scandinavian territory.

Judging from the evidence of place names, Pictish culture and language was largely obliterated in areas occupied by the Vikings. This was, you suspect, probably not accomplished by polite negotiation.

Further Viking attacks struck deep into the heart of the mainland, with dragon-prowed ships sailing up the great rivers such as the Tay and Forth. Ironically, this external threat may have hastened the coming together of the Picts and Scots into the Gaelicised Kingdom of Alba, and thus forming the nucleus of the Scottish state which later bested the Vikings.

Galloway, in the south-west of the country, gets its name from the Gall-Gaidel, a people with a mixed Gaelic-Norwegian ancestry. Even when direct Viking influence waned, the Gall-Gaidel or Norse-Gaels were a force to be reckoned with throughout the islands of the west. For example, in 1164, Somerled, the Norse-Gaelic King of the Isles, invaded Scotland with an army of 15,000 Islesmen – but he was defeated at the Battle of Renfrew by Malcolm IV.

Eleven Viking ship burials have been uncovered in Scotland, the most recent in Ardnarmurchan (Highland/Lochaber), where a man of high status was found buried with his sword, axe, shield and spear beneath an upturned boat 16ft long.

The Battle of Largs (North Ayrshire) in 1263 saw the end of Viking domination, although the Norwegians thought their enemies had not played fair, claiming that Scottish black magicians had raised a destructive storm through sorcery.

The Viking heritage of Shetland is celebrated every January with the Up Helly Aa festival in Lerwick, during which a full-scale Viking longboat is set on fire.

GENE GENIES

More than 150,000 men in Scotland carry within their genes a remarkable ancestry – they are descended from the people who lived in the Ice Age Refuges of southern Europe. With the whole of the north crushed under ice, humanity in Europe survived in small pockets in France, Spain and Italy. When the ice retreated around 12,000 years ago, these people started to walk north – and some ended up in Scotland, the first immigrants to what had previously been a human-free zone. About 6 per cent of Scottish men now have the marker M284 in their DNA – one of the oldest genetic lineages in Europe. Another ancient lineage, M423, which is found in about 20,000 Scottish men, originates from what is now the area around Croatia, Bosnia, Hungary and Romania. Many similar revelations can be found in a book by Alistair Moffat and Dr Jim Wilson, titled *The Scots: A Genetic Journey* (2011).

Every person in Scotland, just like the rest of the population of the world, is ultimately descended from a group of about 5,000 humans who lived in East Africa around 70,000 years ago. In a sense, we are all African.

175,000 Scottish men, mostly in the north and east, are S145-Picts. That is, they carry S145-Pict, the distinctive DNA marker of the Pictish people who largely disappeared from the historic record in the ninth century. In one of the many surprises that DNA studies throw up, over half of the MacGregors tested turned out not to have the DNA of their supposed ancestors, the royal Alpins of Dalriada – that is, the original 'Scots' – but of their neighbours/rivals, the Picts. In addition, around 12 per cent of MacDonalds do carry not the expected Viking marker, but the marker of the Picts. Intriguingly, the MacDonald chiefs of Clan Ranald and MacDonnel of Glengarry are Viking-related – but their followers are S145-Picts. The Picts may have vanished, but their ancient bloodline lives on.

Around 20 per cent of all men in Orkney carry the M17 genetic marker, indicating Viking descent. If the analysis is limited to men with recognised ancient Orcadian surnames – such as Couston, Foubister or Linklater – then the percentage shoots up to 75 per cent.

A sample of forty-five MacLeod men from Skye and the Western Isles showed that almost half were descended from one man – probably Ljot, a Norse aristocrat who is traditionally claimed as the founder of the MacLeod clan.

The DNA marker S145 is found throughout Britain, and the M222 marker is specific to Scotland and Ireland. Both are also found in coastal Norway – almost certainly an indication that the Vikings shipped British slaves back home. Another marker from south-west Ireland turns up in the Western Isles – this is probably the genetic trace of Irish slaves brought north by the Vikings.

The M222 marker originated with one man, Niall Noigiallach, the fifth-century High King of Ulster, who clearly fathered many children with multiple women, as 20 per cent of all Irish men and 6 per cent of all men in Scotland (around 150,000) carry Niall's DNA. Analysis has shown that the M222 marker arrived in Scotland around AD 500 – the period when the tribal Scots of the north of Ireland colonised Argyll, creating the kingdom of Dalriada and introducing the word 'Scot' into the place that was still several centuries away from being called 'Scotland'. Several clans of the west – Campbell, Lamont, MacDowall and MacInnes – have a genetic origin in Ireland.

Around 20,000 modern Scottish men – many of them MacDonalds – are descended from Somerled, the Gaelic-Norse Lord of the Isles who died in 1164. Like Niall Noigiallach, Somerled must have had numerous children with a great many women. Also like Niall, several of his progeny would themselves have been powerful lords, and hence were able to propagate their genes more widely than other men.

What all this says about the status of most women in the Dark and Middle Ages can be summed up in one word: property.

About 10 per cent of Scottish women have one of four genetic lineages – T1a, K2a, J1b1 and mtDNAJ2al – that originate in the area that is now Iraq. It was here in the Fertile Crescent that farming was invented around 11,000 years ago. Peoples bearing this marker migrated through Europe, and some of them arrived in Scotland about 6,000 years ago.

When Welsh Olympic athlete Colin Jackson – whose grandparents arrived from Jamaica – participated in the BBC programme *Who Do You Think You Are?* he discovered that as well as his expected African ancestry, his genetic inheritance was 38 per cent European. Research showed that his great-grandmother was a black maid in the household of a white Scottish plantation owner named Duncan Campbell – who turned out to be Colin Jackson's great-grandfather. Although the maid was not a slave, this episode once again draws attention to the lasting legacy of Scottish involvement in Jamaican slavery.

The history of a nation is never a simple straight line. Power rises and falls. Boundaries expand and shrink. Languages and peoples dominate, and then decline. As its ethnic mix and borders have shifted, Scotland has been Caledonia, Pictland, Dalriada, Alba and Scotia. So the idea that there is an indigenous 'Scottish race' is laughable. Many of the people of Scotland have genetic and cultural roots in Ireland, or north-east or north-west England, or Scandinavia – and those roots stretch back centuries, even millennia. All Scots are immigrants. Like all nations with a history of invasion, colonisation and assimilation, 'Scotland', the land of the Scots, is a country of Heinz peoples – 57 varieties.

MEDIEVAL TIMES

As the Middle Ages progressed, the Gaelic language was replaced over much of Lowland Scotland by English – or, rather, by a version of English known as Scots or Lallans (Lowland Scottish), which in many areas is still the dominant form of speech today. In the north-east, meanwhile, a distinctive variant of Scots evolved called Doric. Today's Scotland is a linguistic patchwork of Gaelic (mostly in the west and north-west), Doric (north-east), the Norse-influenced Shetlandic (Shetland), Scots (Scottish English, widespread) and English (universal).

Scotland's medieval history is as confusing and chaotic as that of any other European nation trying to find its place in the world. The focus these days tends to be on the Wars of Independence fought against an expansionist-minded England – the period of Scottish heroes such as William Wallace and Robert the Bruce – but most battles and conflicts of the period were in fact internal: Scots *v.* Scots. Central authority (the king, often based at Edinburgh or Stirling) was frequently in conflict with other powerbases, such as the noble families, or the clans of the far north and west, or the men of the isles – all of whom would temporarily ally with England if it assisted their grouse with the Scottish king. Internecine warfare between neighbouring clans added

to the misery. Many aristocrats were often little more than titled thugs, and murder, torture, rapine, kidnap and fatal family feuds were very much the order of the day.

Here are a few insights into the cheery and jovial times of medieval Scotland:

King Lulach was assassinated by his successor, Malcolm III, who was in turn killed in battle by an earl whose lands he had devastated.

Duncan II was killed by his own uncle, Donald III.

Robert the Bruce became king by murdering his main rival in a church.

David Stewart, the son and heir of King Malcolm III, was starved to death by his uncle the Duke of Albany.

A cabal of nobles assassinated King James I while he was hiding in a sewer.

Ten-year-old James II was forced to watch the beheading of two members of Clan Douglas, who moments before had been his guests at dinner. As an adult, the king stabbed the Earl of Douglas in the throat.

To give an example of the medieval way of doing things, consider the 1450 Highland clan battle between Cameron of Lochiel and Hector Buie Maclean, Seneschal of Urquhart Castle on Loch Ness. Hector Maclean displayed several murdered and mutilated Cameron hostages from the battlements of Bona Castle, so Cameron of Lochiel responded by hanging two of Maclean's sons in full view of their father.

Or how about the visit to Eilean Donan Castle by the Earl of Moray in 1331: the Mackenzies, keen to show their loyalty, executed no less than fifty men, so that on his arrival the Earl could be greeted by a display of severed heads garlanding the castle walls.

THE CLANS

There are around 350 recognised clan names in Scotland, although the exact figure depends on the arguments between genealogists as to what constitutes a genuine and legally-defined 'clan'.

Clans are found in the Lowlands and Borders as well as the Highlands and Islands.

Well over a hundred modern clans do not have a recognised clan chief, and are known as 'armigerous clans'. Without a chief – the individual who confers noble status on the clan – a clan is unlikely have a solid legal grounding or be regarded as a 'noble corporation'.

That being said, the fine detail of modern clan heraldry and legality is as complex as the past history of clan conflicts. Once, they had warriors; now they have lawyers. Enter at your own risk.

Many clans started as military aristocracies, where power (and land ownership) resided with the strongest of warriors, and the poorer farming classes were bound to the power elite through ties of kinship. The peasants laboured on the land and were duty-bound to fight for the chief when called upon; in return, the chief and his warband were equally duty-bound to protect their people, property and land.

Historically, the elite members of martial aristocracies tend to elevate fighting prowess above all the other virtues. Not surprisingly, then, we find that clan histories are often steeped in blood – especially if the clan was powerful and territorially aggressive. At the lowest level, this could involve the regular purloining of your neighbours' cattle – clan folklore is rife with tales of cattle-raiding by 'caterans'. At the more serious level, a full-scale blood feud could descend into outright warfare and ethnic cleansing. Some major inter-clan disputes, such as those between the MacDonalds and the Campbells, the MacGregors and the Maclarens, or the MacDonalds and the MacLeods, lasted for centuries.

In his book *A Summer in Skye*, author Alexander Smith described the power play between the MacDonalds and the MacLeods on the island thus: 'putting wedding rings on each other's fingers, and dirks into each other's hearts'.

Clan politics constantly shifted: enemies became allies, friends transformed into bitter opponents. Weaker clans – or those that had been decimated in the fighting – sometimes tried to integrate with more powerful clans, a process that often involved a change of name.

After the Battle of Glen Fruin in 1603 – which saw the virtual destruction of the fighting capability of Clan Colquhoun – Clan MacGregor found themselves formally banished by the king. This meant it was illegal to bear the name MacGregor, under pain of death. Some MacGregors promptly became name-only members of Clan Murray or Grant.

During the Jacobite Rebellion of 1745, many people were surprised that the MacLeod and MacDonald clans – the most powerful on Skye, each able to summon hundreds if not thousands of warriors – did not turn out to fight for Bonnie Prince Charlie. The reason was dark and shocking. A few years previously both clan chiefs, finding their tenants both too numerous and insufficiently profitable, had secretly kidnapped many of their own kinsfolk and shipped them off to the New World to be sold as slaves. The ship, however, had put in to an Irish port, where the captives were liberated. The British government threatened to expose both chiefs if they 'came out' for the Pretender. And so, terrified that the truth of their treachery to their own people would destroy their status, the duplicitous leaders of the two great Skye clans told their warriors to stay at home.

The complex web of alliances and enmities that made up the clan system undermines any attempt to construct a simplistic 'us versus them' version of Scottish history. At the Battle of Culloden in 1746, for example, almost a third of the Government troops were from Scottish clans – largely because their traditional clan enemies were fighting for the Jacobite side. And Edward II's 'English' army at the Battle of Bannockburn contained many Scots whose lands had been ravaged by Robert the Bruce. Many dynastic or religious battles in Scottish history have a hidden clan dimension.

The twentieth century saw a new development, with many descendants of the Scottish diaspora visiting Scotland in search of their roots. As a consequence a number of clans now effectively operate as heritage organisations, channelling this enthusiasm into a reworked clan-based culture where past glories are nostalgically celebrated.

THE CLEARANCES

From the late eighteenth century onwards, some clan chiefs started to think of themselves less as protectors of their kinsfolk and more as landlords. To a landlord, a land filled with tenant farmers working marginal fields was far less profitable than a land filled with sheep. As a consequence, large tracts of land in the Highlands and Islands were 'cleared' of people, sometimes with pitiless brutality. Clearances also took place in the Lowlands, although these equally unpleasant cultural vanishing acts have been largely forgotten.

The Clearances forced thousands into emigration. As a result, the United States, Canada, New Zealand, Australia and South Africa all saw massive influxes of Scottish immigrants, many of whom contributed greatly to the cultural and economic dynamism of their adopted homes.

The legacy of the Clearances can be seen everywhere in the Highlands in the form of abandoned villages. A fine one to visit is Badbea, near Ousdale in Caithness (Highland). From 1792 onwards many Caithness families were forcibly cleared from their crofts to make way for sheep, and the only land available to them was this marginal, rough and steeply sloping ground between the new sheep wall and the cliff edge. So grim was the location that children had to be tethered to stakes so that they would not be blown over the steep cliffs. The last inhabitant left in 1911 and the ruins are now maintained as a memorial to the iniquities of the Clearances.

The Clearances continued until the astonishingly late date of 1879, when Alexander Pirie, a wealthy Aberdeen paper magnate, bought the estate of Leckmelm by Loch Broom in Wester Ross (Highland) – and promptly told the twenty-three families living there that they could no longer farm the arable or pasture land that they had worked for generations. The resulting evictions were heartless, with one deaf woman having her house demolished around her, and other families thrown out into the snow – and the resulting row reached Parliament. After many similar incidents across the Highland and Islands, and examples of spirited resistance, the government, through the Crofters' Commission, eventually established security of tenure for crofters and estate tenants. Even up to the 1930s, however, absentee landlords such as the pro-Nazi Baron Brocket, owner of the Knoydart estate, were still pushing crofters around.

Sometimes people were moved on not because they were uneconomic, but because they spoiled the view. On Arran in 1840 Lord Rossmore had the cottages of eighty-five people burned so that his new shooting lodge could have an unrestricted panorama. And in 1803 the Earl of Mansfield demolished the village of Scone in Perth & Kinross and built a replacement 1¾ miles away, thus giving him the space to build his new Scone Palace.

The issue over the use of land continues to blight the Highlands and Islands, especially where ownership rests with a non-resident individual or company whose aims conflict with those of the people who actually live on the land: the populations of the islands of Eigg and Gigha, for example, have both been threatened with mass eviction in recent years. Changes in legislation (and society in general) have seen communities in Assynt, Knoydart and Harris – as well as Gigha and Eigg – take on absentee landlords and purchase the land on which they stand.

EMIGRATION

The Clearances and religious or political persecution aside, most Scots who emigrated chose to make a new life in a new land, especially in the nineteenth century. This led to a number of side effects, not least the demand for mortgages to purchase farms and land overseas. In 1875 the North of Scotland Canadian Mortgage Company was set up in Aberdeen specifically to provide mortgage funds for pioneering Scots families on the Canadian prairies. Other similar companies, in Dundee and elsewhere, were funding the Scottish colonisation of the Wild West, providing mortgages on farms and ranches in Texas, Oklahoma and other American states.

LOVE IS ALL AROUND

The first use of the word 'sweetheart' in the English language dates from 1290, when Lady Devorgilla of Galloway was laid to rest at the abbey she had founded just south of Dumfries. Buried with her was the embalmed heart of her husband Lord John Balliol, which she had carried in a silver casket since his death twenty-two years previously. The Cistercian monks thereafter called the abbey Dulce Cor, or Sweetheart Abbey, by which it is still known today.

A large boulder at Gribun on the Isle of Mull is known as the Tragedy Stone after an event dating from around 1700. A young couple slipped away from their wedding celebrations for the first night in their new cottage – only to be crushed to death by a storm-cracked rock thrust down from the mighty cliffs above. The remains of the tiny dwelling could still be seen poking out from under the boulder 200 years later.

Glasgow, 1780s: James McLehose courts Agnes Craig in defiance of her father's disapproval. McLehose buys all the seats on a stagecoach journey to Edinburgh, so that he and his sweetheart can be alone together in private. Shortly after, they are married – but four years later Agnes leaves James, citing his cruel behaviour towards her.

Overhall Mill, near Sandford, Strathavon (South Lanarkshire), 1801: a local youth courts the miller's daughter. Sent away with a flea in his ear, the lad plots revenge. He clambers up onto the corn mill's thatched roof and angles an eyeglass or pair of spectacles to the sun. Soon the thatch is ablaze, and the mill is gutted. The adjacent waterfall is known as the Spectacle E'e (Eye) Falls.

In 1823 a diary was published entitled "'Statement of Facts', 'Supplement to Statement of Facts', 'Additions to Supplement' and 'The Last'". The author, George Beattie of St Cyrus in Aberdeenshire, did not benefit from the local success of this curious work, as he calmly blew his own brains out just before the book went on sale. The reason for both publication and suicide was simple: his fiancée, having recently received an inheritance, had dumped Beattie for a more upmarket gentleman. As a result of Beattie's post-mortem revenge, the woman – who was named William Gibson because her parents had wanted a son – had to endure the entire district knowing the intimate details of her perfidious love life.

LIFESTYLES OF THE RICH AND FAMOUS

The sumptuous Edwardian country house of Manderston in the Scottish Borders was built to a 'bottomless' budget. As a result it boasts the only silver staircase in the world; cleaning it took three weeks. The basement – which runs for the entire length and breadth of the house – features fifty-six bells, each with a different tone, so that the servants knew which room to head for.

Kinloch Castle, an unbelievably elaborate late-Victorian hunting lodge sitting incongruously on the sparsely inhabited west coast island of Rùm, was the first private residence in Scotland to use electricity. It also has the world's only still-working Orchestrion, an electric-driven organ that plays music from perforated card rolls – a kind of fin-de-siècle synthesizer. The owners – who stayed here for just a few weeks a year – were quite content to spend more than £15 million in today's terms and import 250,000 tons of soil, simply so they could have a nice place to stay when out slaughtering deer (which had also been imported). Colossal wealth + colossal ego = entirely unnecessary colossal mansion on remote island.

When the hugely wealthy 3rd Duke of Sutherland died in 1892, there was a major falling-out between his widow and the rest of the family.

Packed off with a financial settlement and the right to build a castle as long as it was outside the Sutherland lands, the miffed Dowager Duchess duly built Carbisdale Castle on a hill, where it defiantly dominated the view from the Sutherland domain. She even left one of the four sides of the clocktower empty, so that her hated relatives would not even have the time for free. Sadly the 'Castle of Spite', after many years' service as perhaps the most ornate youth hostel in Scotland, is now closed.

In 1562, during the wars of Mary, Queen of Scots, the Protestant Lord James Stewart defeated his loathed enemy George Gordon, the Catholic Earl of Huntly, at the Battle of Corrichie in Aberdeenshire. Huntly, the chief of Clan Gordon, died during the fight – but that was not enough for Stewart, who had the body dressed in sackcloth and taken to Edinburgh, where a court pronounced a verdict of treason over the embalmed remains.

McMAC

The 'Mac' that is often part of Scottish surnames (MacDonald, MacLeod, etc.) is a patronym: it refers to the forename of the person's father and means 'son of' in Gaelic. The English or Scots-English equivalent of MacDonald would be Donaldson, 'the son of Donald'.

'Mac' patronyms are first known from the eleventh century, although the usage changed with successive generations, and it was not until the fifteenth or sixteenth centuries that such names became fixed surnames.

Far less well known is the equivalent female word 'Nic', meaning 'daughter of', which is in use exclusively within Gaelic-speaking communities.

A 'Mac' name does not necessarily indicate a blood relation to the clan chief or even to anyone within the principal clan family. Clan culture was based on the notion of kinship, and 'kin' could include servants, tenants, members of a warband, or incomers from an entirely different clan who farmed the land or simply made allegiance to a powerful clan – and so any of these non-relatives could be 'MacDonalds,' 'MacLeods,' 'MacKinnons' and so on.

In other words, if you have a 'Mac' surname, your distant ancestor is statistically more likely to be a dirt-poor tenant farmer than a famous clan chief.

There is no one correct way to write 'Mac'. Mac, Mc, M'c and M' have all been used, and although the latter two have largely fallen out of use, you will come across them in older documents. Similarly, the question of whether to use a capital letter after the patronym is largely a matter of family preference: both MacKinnon and Mackinnon are correct (as are McKinnon and Mckinnon). The only rule in Scotland is to not put a space between the patronymic and the rest of the name: Mac Kinnon is the Irish usage.

Some 'Mac' names are on the verge of extinction in Scotland, including MacQuoid, MacMicking/McMeekin, and MacCaa.

NAMES

Scottish history provides us with some splendid monikers:

Magnus Barelegs (King of Norway and overlord of much of Scotland, 1073–1103)
Thormod Foal's-leg (twelfth-century Viking pirate)
James of the Fiery Face (King James II, who had a vermillion facial birthmark)
Archibald the Grim (3rd Earl of Douglas, 1328–1400)
Archibald Bell-the-Cat (5th Earl of Angus, 1449–1513)
Alan of the Straws (fifteenth-century pirate)

The two most popular names for modern Scottish babies are Jack and Sophie.

In 2011 the Registrar General recorded the following first names given to babies by parents who may have not been fully thinking things through: Awesome, Boo-Tiger, Cosmos, Delight, Marvelous, Nirvana – and Jesuslovesme.

SAINTS

Fifty men and women from Scotland (or active in the country) have been granted the title 'saint'. The earliest was probably St Ninian, who operated in southern Scotland in the fifth century. However 'Ninian' may actually have been an Irish saint named Finnian of Movilla, but nobody really knows.

Most Scottish saints date from the Dark Ages and the Early Middle Ages, when documentation was sparse, and the reality of their actions (and even their very existence) is often in doubt. In contrast, the most recent saint is John Ogilvie, a Catholic martyred by the Protestants in Glasgow in 1615 – the fulsome records of his trial go into great detail about the tortures he suffered. Ogilvie was canonised by Pope Paul VI in 1976.

Many towns and cities in Scotland have a patron saint. These include St Margaret (Dunfermline); St Mungo (Glasgow); and St Machan (Aberdeen).

The patron saint of Scotland, St Andrew, has no connection with the country whatsoever. One of the Apostles of Jesus, he was a man of the Holy Land. It seems that some of his relics were brought to Scotland in the seventh century, and a combination of myth, political expedience and propaganda eventually created the idea that Andrew was the country's patron saint. The town and the great abbey of St Andrews were named in his honour.

The Dark Ages was the time when several competing kingdoms and peoples competed over territory. Picts, Scots, Anglo-Saxons and Britons all fought each other, or formed alliances of convenience to fight the others. The Battle of Athelstanford in East Lothian in 815 is notable for creating the national flag of Scotland – well, that's the story anyway. The victory of the Scots over the Saxon king Athelstan was supposedly predicted by the appearance of a X-shaped formation of white clouds against the blue sky – the symbol of the cross on which St Andrew was martyred.
  It is possible that elements of this tale may not be entirely true.

Following the victory at Athelstanford, the white-on-blue X-shaped cross, or Saltire, was regarded as the national symbol, and officially became the national flag of Scotland in 1385. The Saltire's white cross on a blue background is now internationally known, partly through Scots painting their face in this manner at sporting events. The face-painting was adopted from a scene in the film *Braveheart*, where William Wallace's army are shown wearing the symbol before a battle.

WITCHES AND WARLOCKS

Stories about Michael Scott, the infamous 'Borders Wizard', are told all over the Scottish Borders. He supposedly trisected a single mountain into the three Eildon Hills above present-day Melrose, and he could foretell the future and command demons. In reality Scott was no sorcerer, but one of the greatest intellectuals of the thirteenth century, a scholar of mathematics and medicine who translated books into Latin from Hebrew and Arabic. At a time when less than 1 per cent of the population could read, Scott's ownership of an actual library filled with mysterious books, many of them foreign, created fear among the superstitious and ignorant – and so his reputation as a 'wizard' was born.

Witchcraft became a capital crime in Scotland in 1563, part of a raft of grim laws introduced by the victorious Protestants of the Reformation, who believed Satan was lurking behind every door. By the time the law was finally repealed in 1735, somewhere between 2,000 and 2,500 people had been executed for witchcraft.

The last execution for witchcraft in the whole of Britain took place in the Highland town of Dornoch in Sutherland in 1727. This was forty-two years after the final witchcraft execution in England.

DEATH

Scotland's first crematorium opened in Glasgow in 1895; it was only the third crematorium in the UK. Fin-de-siècle Scotland didn't take to

the idea quickly, and only 191 cremations were carried out in the first decade. These days, the majority of funerals involve cremation.

The gravestone of John Taylor in Leadhills, South Lanarkshire, claims that he was 137 years old when he died in 1770. This calculation was based on his memory of a total eclipse of the sun in 1652, when he was supposedly 19 years of age. Although Taylor was undoubtedly extraordinarily old, it is unlikely he had attained the age ascribed to him. The longest-lived person on record was a Frenchwoman who died in 1997 at the age of 122.

TALL AND MIGHTY

You can't go far in Scottish folklore without bumping into stories of giants. Sometime in the nineteenth century, for example, two enormous human skeletons were supposedly dug up near Glen Bernera in Lochalsh (Highland). According to Otta Swire's 1963 book *The Highlands and their Legends*, a doctor on the scene pronounced that the bones belonged to men who were precisely 8½ft and 11ft tall!

One giant we know existed was Angus MacAskill, who was born on Berneray in the Western Isles in 1825, and reached the height of 7ft 8in. *The Guinness Book of Records* regards MacAskill as the tallest 'true' giant in recorded history, inasmuch as he was simply a normal man with the usual proportions of an adult male, and did not suffer from any growth abnormality. A life-size figure can be admired in the Giant MacAskill Museum at Dunvegan on Skye.

In about 1850, local strongman Angus Graham moved a large boulder on Barvas moor on Lewis in the Western Isles. The boulder is still there, and although no one really knows how much it weighs, it is probably more than a ton. Graham may have been the strongest man in Britain at the time.

In 1860 Donald Dinnie of Birse in Aberdeenshire simultaneously carried two boulders with a combined weight of 734lbs from one wall of a bridge to another, an astonishing feat. Dinnie went on to become a 'superstar' of nineteenth-century athletics. The stones are still there, outside the Potarch Hotel near Banchory, and have been lifted by a number of strongmen in recent years, including Dave Prowse – who, depending on your vintage, you might know as the Green Cross Code Man, or possibly Darth Vader.

EXPLORERS

Unexplored Africa called to several Scottish souls. David Livingstone, we presume, came from Blantyre in South Lanarkshire. The earlier adventurer Mungo Park was born in Selkirk (Scottish Borders), and James Bruce, 'the Abyssinian Traveller' who found the source of the Blue Nile in 1770, originated from Kinnaird in Stirling District. Livingstone and Park both died in Africa, while Bruce's accounts of his travels were dismissed as fantasy at the time, and he retired to his country house in a huff.

Mungo Park has memorials in Selkirk and Peebles (where he practiced as a doctor) while the David Livingstone Centre in Blantyre is located in the tenement where the explorer-missionary was born.

Far less well known is Joseph Thomson of Penpont in Dumfries & Galloway, who led seven expeditions into Africa between 1878 and 1892. A large mammal, Thomson's Gazelle, is named after him, while H. Rider Haggard lifted parts of Thomson's 1885 book *Through Masai Land* and incorporated them into his bestselling novel *King Solomon's Mines*.

A plaster copy of the Rosetta Stone is built into the entrance lobby of a house in Peebles. It was installed by Thomas Young, the medical officer who served with the 1801 expedition to the Nile during which the famous stone was secured. The original Rosetta Stone, of course, is in the British Museum; just to complicate matters, it was first deciphered by another Dr Thomas Young, although this one was an English polymath, and no relation.

KINGS AND QUEENS

If you want historical accuracy, you can throw William Shakespeare's *Macbeth* out of the window. Duncan, the old king who Macbeth murders in the play, was actually a youngish man who led an invasion into Macbeth's local powerbase in Moray. When Macbeth killed Duncan in battle in 1040, he assumed the kingship, as was normal. And in contrast to the bloodthirsty tyrant of legend, Macbeth was, at least by the standards of medieval kings, not too dreadful. Furthermore, Birnam Wood did not come to Dunsinane; Macbeth was killed not at Dunsinane in Perthshire, but at Lumphanan in Aberdeenshire.

Alexander II (1198–1249) became king at the age of 16 and reigned for an impressive thirty-five years. In 1232, however, it looked as if his life would be cut short by illness. A surgeon, Neis de Ramsay, performed what might have been the first recorded abdominal operation in Europe, and cut out what was described as a trichinbezoar (hairball) from the king's stomach. Neis was rewarded with the estate of Bamff near Alyth in Perth & Kinross, and the Ramsay family continue to hold the lands to this day. In 1534 a boundary stone was recorded on the border of the estate at Bamff: it shows not just Neis' surgical shears, but also the royal hairball.

Over a dozen places in Scotland state 'Mary, Queen of Scots slept here,' including Stirling, Jedburgh, Borthwick, St Andrews and Hermitage Castle. This is just the tip of the iceberg, however, as Mary travelled extensively through her kingdom, mostly on horseback, and the abysmal state of the roads was such that overnight stops were usually short hops apart. Mary slept at fifteen castles owned

by the Crown, twenty-two abbeys and bishop's palaces, thirty-four houses and castles occupied by the great nobles, fifty properties owned by lesser lairds, seventeen townhouses or similar dwellings in towns or burghs, and at least four other buildings which cannot now be identified. That makes a minimum of 142 places that can claim 'Mary, Queen of Scots slept here.'

There have been seven Scottish kings named James, all of them from the House of Stuart. And to the confusion of visitors and history students everywhere, there were two kings named James I.

James I of Scotland was a medieval monarch, king from 1406 to 1437. Fast-forward to the Renaissance era and 1567: following the abdication of his mother Mary, Queen of Scots, the infant James Stuart became the sixth in a line of Scottish kings named James. Then in 1603, on the death of Elizabeth I, James VI of Scotland inherited the English throne. As England and Scotland were still two separate countries, this king was therefore known as James I of England and James VI of Scotland. The 'Union of the Crowns' in 1603 was followed by the 'Union of Parliaments' in 1707, when Scotland and England became the same state.

James I of England and VI of Scotland made several major impacts on history, including the colonisation of the New World and the commissioning of the King James Bible. As a consequence, if a general history book produced from an English or American perspective mentions James I, almost certainly it is talking about the early seventeenth-century James I of England and VI of Scotland, rather than the less well-known fifteenth-century James I of Scotland.

Also guaranteed to cause confusion is the last Stuart king, who was James II in England and, simultaneously, James VII in Scotland.

Royalty in Medieval and Renaissance Scotland suffered a persistent problem: munchkin monarchs. Time and again kings (and queens) died young or were forced to abdicate, leaving the throne to a child. This inevitably required the appointment of regents to rule the kingdom until the child came of age and regents, being the most powerful people in the kingdom, were not surprisingly often loath to give up that power. Puissant families warred amongst each other to grab the job of regent, while queen regents were often the puppet of one or other competing factions.

Regents, Guardians or Governors were appointed for the childhoods of Alexander II, David II, James I, James II, James III, James V, James VI, and Mary, Queen of Scots.

King James III was killed at the Battle of Sauchieburn near Stirling in 1488. The standard story says that having been injured, the king was taken to a nearby mill, where he was treacherously assassinated by a man disguised as a priest. In reality James was probably killed during or just after the battle, while the 'murder in the barn' story is an invention of later writers. The winner at Sauchieburn (Stirling District) was, by the way, James' own 15-year-old son. For the twenty-five years of his reign, King James IV, as the boy became, wore a heavy iron chain wrapped around his skin, as an act of contrition for his role in the death of his father.

James IV, who died in 1513 fighting the English at the Battle of Flodden Field in Northumberland, was the last king anywhere in Britain to be killed in battle.

James VI and I tried to raise some extra finance for his coffers by creating a new order of chivalry. The Order of the Knights of the Golden Mines would be conferred on anyone rich enough (and foolhardy enough) to invest in the dubious benefits of Scotland's meagre gold mines. The idea didn't catch on.

Another of James' money-raising ideas was the selling of titles. Hand over enough cash, and you could be a Baronet of Nova Scotia ('New Scotland') in Canada, entitled to use 'Sir' before your name. Although the colonisation scheme ultimately failed, the Baronetage of Nova Scotia was a nice little earner for the king.

The realpolitik of seventeenth-century Britain was brutally simple: England was richer and had greater political and military clout than Scotland. To argue otherwise is similar to claiming that the UK today is on a par with the USA. Once James VI of Scotland had acceded to the throne of England in 1603, he never once returned north of the border – indeed, he was dazzled at the wealth of his English subjects. The succeeding Stuart kings shared his feelings. Charles I, who spent the first three and a half years of his life in Dunfermline in Fife, only reluctantly returned to Scotland in 1633 for his Scottish coronation, and thereafter his time in the country was dictated by warfare alone, during the period of the Covenanters and the Civil War. Charles II used the Scots as a stepping-stone to power; once he was enthroned in London, he never again returned to Scotland.

Charles II was last on Scottish soil in 1650. After that, no reigning British monarch set foot in Scotland until 1822, when George IV made his celebrated grand visit to Edinburgh.

The royal neglect of Scotland changed forever with Queen Victoria. Anxious to visit every part of her kingdom, and enraptured by Sir Walter Scott's romantic version of Scotland, she first visited the country in 1842, and returned many times thereafter.

In 1852 the queen and Prince Albert purchased the Balmoral estate near Crathie in Highland Aberdeenshire. Balmoral Castle remains the summer home of the Royal Family, and not surprisingly is one of the more popular tourist destinations in the area.

Victoria's enduring passion for all things Scottish had a major economic impact, as it made both Scottish products and holidaying in Scotland increasingly fashionable. The English landed classes found Scottish estates were ideal for hunting, shooting and fishing – ideal because the land had been emptied of people by the Highland Clearances.

The Queen of Handa was the title given to whoever was the oldest widow living on the tiny island of Handa, off the west coast of Sutherland (Highland). Members of the island's twelve families met daily in a form of parliament, and deferred to the queen as their leader. The islanders all left in 1848 and Handa is now a nature reserve, playing host to 100,000 seabirds in the summer.

3

FROM LOCHS & RIVERS TO SHIPS & THE SEA

RIVERS

You can argue that much of Scotland's history and human geography is shaped, not by mountains and plains, but by rivers. Stirling (and indeed the mighty fortress of Stirling Castle) owes its very location to being the lowest spot downriver where, during the Middle Ages, a bridge could be built over the River Forth. Whoever controlled that bridge controlled the main route between the Lowlands and the Highlands. A similar reason lies behind Perth's very specific location on the River Tay, a strategic fact recognised by the Romans when they built a bridge there.

The River Clyde, which flows through Glasgow, was once too shallow and reef-bound for major ships. The dredging and clearing of the river – which took over a century – created a waterway so vast it enabled Glasgow to become an industrial and trading metropolis. 'Glasgow made the Clyde and the Clyde made Glasgow' is not just a saying, but a veritable truth.

Rivers have frequently marked borders. The border between England and Scotland has often been set by the Tweed in the east (exiting into the sea at Berwick-upon-Tweed) and the River Esk and Solway Firth in the west above Carlisle. Even today, after centuries of boundary changes, both rivers still form some parts of the border.

Much of the centre of Aberdeen, including the railway station and the shopping complex of Union Square, was once beneath the waters of the River Dee; the land was reclaimed by a mighty engineering project in the nineteenth century.

In October 1637 a great flood of rainwater poured out from the River Dee and pushed four ships riding at anchor in Aberdeen harbour far out to sea, smashing a military transport to smithereens and drowning ninety-two soldiers.

The River Spey in the north-east supports twenty-five whisky distilleries, making it the world's unrivalled 'whisky river'.

The water level of the Falls of Clyde in South Lanarkshire is normally controlled by the nearby power station. The station is closed for maintenance on a few days a year – which provides the opportunity for what are called Waterfall Days, when the full force of the 92ft falls at Corra Linn can be appreciated.

Waterways are so important in the history and culture of Scotland that they have developed a wide variety of names:

An estuary is a 'firth', such as the Firth of Forth, the estuary of the River Forth.

A minor river is often called a 'water', as in Edinburgh's Water of Leith, which few people who live in the city know exists.

'Burn' is the name for anything from a small stream to a moderate river. Bannockburn is just one of many places that takes its name from a watercourse. The Gaelic word for burn is Allt, and you will find many examples in the Highlands and Islands, such as Allt Camghouran, which flows into Loch Rannoch. The oft-seen 'Allt Mor' (or Mhor) means 'big burn'.

Also common is 'Abhainn', Gaelic for river, although it is never used for a major river. To confuse matters, sometimes the words 'river' and 'Abhainn' are used for different parts of the same waterway. Gruinard River, in the north-west Highlands, for example, is known in its upper reaches as Abhainn na Clach Airigh.

You will also find 'lade', a word signifying a man-made watercourse that carries water to a mill. St Andrews has a famous lade-side walk, the Lade Braes, while Perth's Town Lade not only powered several mills but also provided a defensive moat around the medieval town.

Sometime in the first half of the seventeenth century, a religious fanatic named Peter Mackie announced that he could walk on water. A large crowd gathered to watch his attempt to stroll across the River Tay at Perth; the mighty river, however, did not share Mr Mackie's belief in his powers, and the would-be miracle worker abandoned the attempt just as the waters reached his mouth.

At 115 miles in length, the Tay is Scotland's longest river, running from Highland Perthshire to the sea beyond Dundee. And although six other rivers in England and Wales are longer, the Tay is the largest river in the UK by volume of discharge.

The shortest Scottish river is on the Isle of Skye, where the River Scavaig runs for little more than 250 yards from Loch Coruisk to the sea.

The shortest river name in Scotland (and Europe) is the River E, which flows south-east of Loch Ness into Loch Mhòr. It shares the 'shortest name' title with the D River in the USA.

CANALS

Driven by the increasing urgency of the industrial revolution and the need for the movement of goods, people and raw materials, work started on Scotland's first canal in 1768. In a story that became all too familiar in later years – and is even truer with today's engineering projects – the project went vastly over budget and vastly over schedule. In fact it took twenty-two years before the 35-mile long Forth & Clyde Canal was opened for business for cross-Scotland traffic between Maryhill in Glasgow and the River Forth on the east coast.

In the meantime, a far less ambitious but more focused canal had been doing very nicely, thank you. At 2¼ miles in length, the Stevenston Canal served the coalfields of North Ayrshire, and had opened in 1772, making it the first operating commercial canal in Scotland.

Other Scottish canal projects included:
The Monklands Canal, between the coalmines of Monklands and Glasgow (finally opened, after many delays, 1794);
The Aberdeenshire Canal, from Aberdeen to Inverurie (opened 1805);
The Crinan Canal in Argyll, a short cut from Loch Fyne to the sea, thus avoiding the long trek around the Mull of Kintyre (opened 1809);
The Glasgow, Paisley & Johnstone Canal (opened 1810/1811, and the scene of one of the first mass canal tragedies, with eighty-four people drowning in what became known as the Paisley Canal Disaster);

The Dingwall Canal, a mile-long tidal canal to the Cromarty Firth (opened 1819);
The Union Canal, linking Edinburgh with the Forth & Clyde Canal and hence Glasgow (opened 1822);
The Forth & Cart Canal, a mere half-mile of water linking the Forth & Clyde Canal to the River Clyde in Glasgow (opened 1840);
And the Caledonian Canal, passing from Inverness to Fort William through the Great Glen and its four lochs (finally opened 1847, after forty-four years of work).

Most of the canals were bedevilled by engineering and financial problems, and then by changing social and economic factors. The Stevenston Canal, for example, closed in the 1830s when the coalfields it served were exhausted. The interlinked Forth & Clyde and Union Canals were out-competed by the introduction of the railways from the 1840s. After less than fifty years in existence, the Aberdeenshire Canal was drained and its route used by a railway in 1854. And the Caledonian Canal took so long to build that by the time it opened, the new generation of steamships was too large to use the canal.

As well as twenty-nine locks, the Caledonian Canal passes through numerous road bridges, many of which have to be swung open to let the boats manoeuvre past. All of the lock and bridge mechanisms were converted to hydraulic power in the 1960s – all except one. At Moy, near Gairlochy, the bridge keeper still has to open the swing bridge by hand, an operation which, to this day, requires him to first cross the canal in a small rowboat.

In 1859 a reservoir dam burst and inundated the Crinan Canal, creating a huge wave that pulverised the canalside in both directions.

Several canals were closed to traffic in the years after the Second World War, and lay abandoned and neglected. In recent years these waterways have been recognised as a unique combination of industrial and natural heritage, and have been rejuvenated.

Four canals are now open for water traffic: the Forth & Clyde Canal and the Union Canal, joined together by the high-tech boat-lift of the Falkirk Wheel; the Crinan Canal; and the magnificent Caledonian Canal, one of the great waterway routes of the world, passing through Loch Ness and a feast of Highland scenery. The Monkland Canal, meanwhile, is no longer navigable but it still provides the main water supply for the Forth & Clyde Canal.

LOCHS

The word 'loch', meaning a body of water, sounds like a good Scots word; in fact it is borrowed from Gaelic.

Only one natural body of water in Scotland is given the name of 'lake' – the Lake of Menteith in Stirling District, which for an obscure reason ceased to be called the Loch of Menteith sometime in the nineteenth century. There are also four artificial reservoirs or ornamental water bodies designated as lakes.

A small loch is known as a lochan.

North-east of Blair Atholl in Perth & Kinross is a body of water called Loch Loch.

There are well over 31,000 freshwaters lochs in Scotland, plus some 200 sea lochs; no one uses the word 'fjord' for the sea lochs, but that is what most of them are.

The largest freshwater loch by surface area is Loch Lomond; the largest by volume is Loch Ness. Loch Ness holds more water than all the lakes of England and Wales put together.

Loch Ness is also the second deepest loch (Loch Morar in Lochaber, Highland, is deeper in places, with some sections plunging to over a 1,000ft deep).

No large aquatic animal can live permanently in Loch Ness because the loch is a low-nutrient environment: quite simply, there is not enough to eat. If there is a Loch Ness Monster, it can only be an occasional visitor from the sea.

In 1870 a hunt for another water monster, the mythical human-eating water horse, took place in the small Loch nan Dubhrachan on the Isle of Skye. A net was dragged the whole length of the loch – when it got stuck halfway across, most people present ran away because they feared the water horse had been caught. As it happened, the net merely captured two fish and a fine collection of mud.

In 1784 Loch Tay (Perth & Kinross), the sixth largest loch in the country, sloshed around like tea in a saucer, at one point drawing back in a great wave and exposing 100 yards of loch-bed.

Crannogs – artificial island dwellings dating from as far back as the Iron Age – are found on many lochs. The Crannog Centre on Loch Tay has a fully reconstructed island crannog made of wood and thatch.

THE SEA

The nature of Scotland's indented coastline, with sea lochs reaching deep into the body of the country, means that the total length of coast is over 7,300 miles – the distance from Edinburgh to Jakarta in Indonesia.

No matter where you are in Scotland, you are never more than 41 miles from salt water.

About 8,000 species of plants and animals live in the seas around Scotland.

There are cold-water corals off Mingulay in the Western isles and worm reefs in Loch Creran, Argyll.

Approximately 71 per cent of all the sand dunes in Britain are found in Scotland.

Scotland's seas are already experiencing climate change. The temperature has increased by more than 0.2°C every decade since 1985. In terms of sea level, one of the highest rises has been at Aberdeen, where the average sea level is now 4in higher than it was 100 years ago.

The highest tidal range in Scotland occurs in the inner Solway Firth, where high water and low water during the spring tides can differ by between 23 and 26ft.

The lowest tidal range is found between Islay and the Mull of Kintyre.

Europe's first long distance kayak trail stretches from Gigha off the coast of Argyll to the Summer Isles north-west of Loch Broom and Ullapool (Highland). The route takes three weeks to complete.

FISHER FOLK

Aberdeen was established as a major fish-curing centre by the eleventh century. In 1081 King Edward I of England sent his quartermaster to the port, where he purchased 100 barrels of sturgeons as part of the food supplies for an army about to invade Wales.

In 1696 the money-minded landowner of Foveran in Aberdeenshire insisted that three fisherman who lived on his estates were duty-bound to work for him alone, and not for any other client, boat or fleet. The Court of Session disagreed, stating that to confine fishermen in this manner was tantamount to slavery.

In 2008 the marine sector – principally fishing and related activities – contributed £3.6 billion to the Scottish economy, or around 3.5 per cent of the total economic value of the country.

For anyone intrigued by the mysterious names read out on each day's shipping forecast, 'Bailey' is the sea area north of Rockall and far to the west of the Western Isles, while 'Forties' is the area in the North Sea well beyond the east coast.

PIRATES

Any seafaring nation has a pirate or two lurking in the less respectable corners of its history. Piracy was a major problem in the Hebrides during the sixteenth century. The Gaelic name for the island of Longay near Skye means 'pirate ship,' and a hidden harbour on Rona was known as Port nan Robaireann ('the robbers' port'). Clan MacNeil of Barra in the Western Isles were inveterate pirates.

Contrary to the romanticised glamour cast over piracy by the movies, pirate life tended to involve murder, torture, enslavement, and the kidnap and rape of women. All these factors were present in the career of John Gow, the 'Orkney Pirate,' who was hanged in London in 1725, having started his life as a pirate by leading a mutiny and murdering his captain.

The most famous Scottish pirate was Captain Kidd. Dundee-born William Kidd may or may have not been an actual pirate, and may or may not have been betrayed by a cabal of Government toffs who had used him for their own semi-legal purposes. In any case, he was actually a minor player in piracy terms – his fame rests on the vast but possibly mythical treasure that he allegedly left behind him, the location of which has defeated generations of treasure hunters.

One sailor from Perth led perhaps the most unusual life of any Scottish pirate. Peter Lisle was a deckhand on the American schooner *Betsy* when it was captured by Barbary Corsairs, the infamous pirates operating out of North and West Africa under the protection of the Ottoman Empire. As was usual, his new masters worked Lisle as a slave. What was unexpected was that he converted to Islam, became the new captain of the *Betsy*, led multiple attacks on American and European vessels, and rose to the rank of the Grand Admiral of the Tripoli Navy – and the son-in-law of the local ruler to boot. Lisle – or Murad Reis as he was now known – died a violent death in 1832, having been a Barbary Corsair for thirty-five years.

SAFETY AT SEA

Scotland's first permanently manned coal-fired warning beacon was set up on the Isle of May in the Firth of Forth in 1635. In 1791 a light keeper, his wife and five of their children were suffocated to death by fumes from the beacon.

The construction of lighthouses around Scotland's rocky and dangerous coast was a heroic undertaking. The first proper lighthouses were built at Kinnaird Head (Aberdeenshire) and the Mull of Kintyre (Argyll) in 1787. In 1824 Robert Stevenson published *An Account of the Bell Rock Light-House*, which went into hair-raising detail of the perils involved in the three-year construction of a 115ft lighthouse on a sea-washed reef that was underwater for twenty hours out of every twenty-four.

When the Bell Rock light was switched on in 1810 it was the tallest offshore lighthouse in the world. It is still there, 11 miles off the coast of Angus; the 200-year-old masonry has never needed replacing.

Bell Rock communicated with the mainland via flags visible from the Signal Tower in Arbroath (Angus). For worried expectant fathers on the lighthouse, the Signal Tower hoisted a special set of signals on the flagstaff – a pair of trousers to show that a boy had been delivered, and a petticoat for a girl.

The first automated lighthouse in Scotland was established as early as 1894, when Oxcars Lighthouse near Granton (Edinburgh) was run on gas controlled by a clockwork timer. A boatman brought the gas from Granton Gasworks once a week – and also had to wind up the timer.

Fair Isle South, the last manned lighthouse in Scotland, was automated in 1998.

The northernmost light in Scotland is on Muckle Flugga, a rock off the coast of Unst in Shetland. A good (if windy) view of the lighthouse can be obtained from the nearby bird reserve on Unst.

The lighthouse at Cape Wrath (Caithness/Highland), despite being on the mainland, was accorded Rock (offshore) status in 1977. The change came about in recognition of the difficulty in reaching the location by road, and allowed supplies to be delivered by helicopter.

Her Majesty's Coastguard co-ordinate maritime search and rescue operations for British coastlines and waters. Following a controversial set of changes in 2010, there are now only three coastguard stations in Scotland: Aberdeen, Shetland, and Stornoway on the Western Isles. The Firth of Clyde, Scotland's busiest waterway, is managed by the Belfast coastguard.

In 2012 Aberdeen coastguard were called out seventy-three times, an increase of 93 per cent over the previous year.

One of the most arduous rescues undertaken by the Stornoway coastguard took place in 1953, when all sixty-six crew members were successfully taken off the SS *Clan Macquarrie*, which had run aground off Lewis in storm conditions, where the wind was over 115mph.

A very small number of calls to the coastguard are false alarms. In October 2008 flashing lights were seen in the sea off Staffin on the Isle of Skye. When the coastguard investigated, they found a tiny toy boat bearing the message 'Happy 42nd Birthday Ollie xxx'.

The Royal National Lifeboat Institution (RNLI) has forty-five all-volunteer lifeboat stations around Scotland, along with an inland station at Loch Ness.

Twenty-seven RNLI lifeboatmen have lost their lives during operations in Scottish waters; the last fatality was in 1970, when five members of the Fraserburgh (Aberdeenshire) lifeboat drowned.

SHIPS NAMED SCOTLAND

The first SS (Steam Ship) named *Scotland* was a three-masted passenger steamer built in Jarrow in 1865, and at the time regarded as the most advanced transatlantic steamer of the age. After just a year in service she collided with another ship off Fire Island near New York, the wreck posing a threat to vessels entering the channel into New York Harbour. A lightship, the *Wreck of Scotland* (later just called the *Scotland*) marked the site and kept the route safe.

The second SS *Scotland* was a large iron-hulled steamship built in 1869 at Kinghorn in Fife. Having had a full life taking troops to India and emigrants to Canada, she was scrapped in the 1890s.

The *Scotland* was a Danish schooner lost off Iceland in 1904. That same year the third SS *Scotland* was launched at Grangemouth in West Lothian. In 1911 the Norwegian-owned cargo ship was lost after running aground off Langesund in Norway.

Another Norwegian SS *Scotland* cargo vessel was less than four years old when in 1916 it ran aground off the Isle of May in the Firth of Forth. The wreck is still on the seabed.

The FV (Fishing Vessel) *Scotland* was a Hull steam trawler built in 1897. In 1919 she hit a mine left over from the First World War and sank off the Yorkshire coast. Yet another SS *Scotland* was lost in the same area in 1920, this one a dredger that capsized near Bridlington.

The MSC (Mediterranean Shipping Company) *Scotland* is a dry goods container ship commissioned in 1992, and still afloat.

Although the Royal Navy once had both a destroyer and a submarine named HMS *Scotsman*, there have been no ships called HMS *Scotland*. The present-day HMS *Scotia* is not actually a ship, but a shore-based Royal Naval Reserve unit.

4

WARS, BATTLES & REBELLIONS

BACK IN THE BAD OLD DAYS

In AD 84 the Roman army defeated a confederation of Caledonian tribes at the great battle of Mons Graupius. No one can agree where the battle actually took place – there are at least a dozen candidates for the location, mostly in Aberdeenshire. The only Roman account of the battle, which may be fictional in places, says the Caledonian chieftain was named Calgacus, and that he gave a rousing speech to his troops just before battle commenced – a speech worthy of the best Roman senator. Of course, Calgacus made no such speech; he may not even have existed, and even if he had, the Romans would not have been able to understand him. Still, it has created one of the most-quoted lines on the futility of war – 'They make a desert and call it peace.'

THERE GOES THE NEIGHBOURHOOD

Once both England and Scotland became established as fully fledged nations in the early Middle Ages, fighting periodically erupted between the neighbours. To understand the nature of the conflicts, a little insight into medieval politics is required. The Norman invasion of 1066 had made England a feudal state, where the king granted tracts of lands to aristocratic warriors, who in turn were duty-bound to provide military service to the king, bringing with them as many troops as they could raise. Feudalism was introduced into Scotland 1124 by King David I, who himself owned large tracts of land in southern England. For a noble, success in war brought gifts from the king in terms of more land, and hence more wealth. And wealthy nobles could provide more troops. Both Scottish and English kings therefore had a vested interest in acquiring more territory. It is also the reason why, throughout the Middle Ages, Scottish nobles would ally with the English crown against the Scottish king if they thought this gave them an advantage. Power and privilege (and money) speaks more strongly than patriotism.

Even Scottish kings were happy to engage in a bit of English argy-bargy. In 1215 the English barons rose up against King John, and Alexander II of Scotland decided to join in by allying with their cause. Having invaded Cumbria and Northumberland, he then rode to Dover to pledge fealty to Louis Capet, the heir to the French throne and the barons' choice to replace John. Sadly for Alexander's designs on expanding the territory of the Kingdom of Scotland across northern England, his alliance with the English nobles came to naught: John died, the barons switched their allegiance to the king's eldest son Henry III, and Alexander was out in the cold.

Added to all this feudal land-grabbing was the simple issue of resources. Enlarging your territory meant more land for crops, sheep and cattle, and more natural resources such as timber or iron. And then there was the question of ports. Every medieval nation needed safe harbours for trade (and therefore wealth), and for the transport of troops during times of war. All this explains why so much blood was spilled over the location of the border between the two neighbours, and why the Borders port of Berwick-upon-Tweed changed hands so many times.

To complicate matters, the Border area was remote from the centres of kingly power in both England and Scotland, so that local warlords could often act with impunity. For centuries, the area which is now the Scottish Borders and the eastern part of Dumfries & Galloway (and Cumbria and Northumberland in England), was disputed land, where cross-border raids were often little to do with international warfare and more an expression of the unruly bandits who brought death and destruction to both sides of the divide. The Border clans frequently joined in with more organised warfare – on either the Scottish or the English side – partly as this gave them the opportunity for more plunder.

We also encounter the age-old political gamble known as 'my enemy's enemy is my friend'. England had more resources than the far less populated Scotland, and so the latter needed allies. Norway, rapaciously eating away at Scotland's northern and western fringes, was out of the question. Neither Wales nor Ireland had the requisite organisation or political will, and both then fell to Norman dominion. The only remaining candidate was France, which was then much smaller than it is now. A pact was signed between the two countries in 1295, and the 'Auld Alliance' continued to play a part in Scottish politics for centuries.

Then again, international wars were sometimes a consequence of power struggles within Scotland – Duncan II, for example, came to the Scottish throne in 1094 by invading his homeland with the help of the army of William II of England.

THEY CAN NEVER TAKE OUR FREEDOM!

It was a similar internal power struggle that led to the most celebrated period of the Scottish battle saga, the First War of Scottish Independence, which saw, for the first time, England seeking to conquer Scotland entirely. For fifty years from 1296 onwards, three successive English kings – Edward I, Edward II and Edward III – attempted to bring Scotland to heel. The fortunes of both sides swung back and forth. The enduring folk hero William Wallace scored a resounding victory over the English in 1297 at the Battle of Stirling Bridge, only to

suffer a major defeat the following year. From 1306 Robert the Bruce fought a guerrilla campaign that eventually culminated in the triumph of the Battle of Bannockburn in 1314 – but it took another fourteen years before Scotland's independence was formally recognised.

The first blood at the Battle of Bannockburn was a single combat between Robert the Bruce and the English knight Henry de Bohun; Bruce's battleaxe split de Bohun's head in two.

The Wars of Independence were both an international conflict and a civil war. In 1306 Robert the Bruce had murdered his principal rival, the Red Comyn, during negotiations in a church. The Scottish nobles who opposed Bruce then had their estates burned and their people slaughtered – Galloway, Argyll, Buchan, Strathspey and many other areas suffered terribly. Not surprisingly, these nobles thirsted for revenge. At the Battle of Bannockburn perhaps 10 per cent of the English army were made up of the Scots who hated Bruce, and after Bruce died, the aggrieved Scottish nobles invaded Scotland, calling upon England for assistance. This in turn prompted the Second War of Independence (1332–1357), which ended only because England became too preoccupied with wars in France.

Robert the Bruce and the Battle of Bannockburn have iconic cultural and political status within Scotland, and the battlefield became an early commemorative focus for the Scottish National Party. Bruce's murder of his rival in a holy sanctuary, his merciless harrying of the estates of his Scottish enemies, and the significant Scottish presence opposing him at Bannockburn – all these tend to be forgotten or brushed over.

Also largely forgotten is the Scottish invasion of Ireland, where Robert the Bruce's brother Edward led an ill-thought-out campaign against the Anglo-Irish aristocracy. Many Irish detested their English overlords, so prospects initially looked good; but Bruce's troops behaved so badly that the Irish regarded them as a worse curse than the English.

WE ARE THE CHAMPIONS

Not surprisingly, Scottish popular history tends to prefer the battles where the Scots won, a theme that is also followed by filmmakers, owners of castles, nostalgic romantics, and re-enactors of medieval battles. For the record, here are the battles between Scotland and England, all of which were won by England. Strangely enough, these are somehow less celebrated north of the border.

Northallerton, 1138 (Scotland invaded England)
Alnwick, 1174 (Scotland invaded England – William I of Scotland captured)
Dunbar, 1296 (England invaded Scotland)
Falkirk, 1298 (England invaded Scotland – William Wallace defeated)
Methven, 1306 (England invaded Scotland – Robert the Bruce defeated)
Halidon Hill, 1333 (Scotland invaded England – Berwick captured)

Neville's Cross, 1346 (Scotland invaded England – David II of Scotland captured)
Nesbit Moor, 1402 (Scotland invaded England)
Humbleton Hill, 1402 (Scotland invaded England)
Flodden, 1513 (Scotland invaded England – James IV of Scotland killed)
Solway Moss, 1542 (Scotland invaded England – led indirectly to the death of James V of Scotland)
Pinkie Cleugh, 1547 (England invaded Scotland)

It's fair to say that on about the same number of occasions, the Scots were victorious, with standout successes at Loudon Hill (1307, Robert the Bruce), Byland Moor (1322, Robert the Bruce), Stanhope Park (1327) and Otterburn (1388). Even so, looking at the statistics, it would appear that it was on average not a good idea for Scotland to invade England.

BONJOUR, MCMONSIEUR

What's the greatest Scottish military victory over England? The Battle of Stirling Bridge in 1297, which saw an army led by William Wallace use brilliant tactics to defeat a numerically superior force? The Battle of Bannockburn in 1314, when Robert the Bruce crushed the army of Edward II? Or the Battle of Baugé?

Unless you're an expert on the Hundred Years' War, you've probably never heard of the Battle of Baugé. You might be slightly more familiar with the 1415 Battle of Agincourt (famously celebrated in Shakespeare's *Henry V*), in which English forces crushed the French army and started to retake northern France as an English possession. Faced with the eclipse of their kingdom, the French turned for help to England's other enemy – Scotland. In 1419 about 6,000 Scottish mercenaries decamped for France, and the 'Army of Scotland' became the strong right arm of French military strategy. In 1421, at Baugé in western France, the Scots wiped the floor with the English, killing the Duke of Clarence, who was Henry V's brother and the heir to the English throne. Baugé probably saved the French kingdom from extinction.

The victorious Scots were showered with rewards – titles, lands, bishoprics and money – much to the despair of the peasantry, who were forced to support these foreigners who insisted on eating and drinking only the best France had to offer.

The good times were not to last, however. In 1423 a Franco-Scottish army led by Sir John Stewart of Darnley was flattened at the Battle of Cravant by an alliance between England and the Duchy of Burgundy: perhaps 3,000 Scots were killed. The following year, even with an additional 6,500 troops freshly arrived from Scotland, the English were again triumphant. The Battle of Verneuil in Normandy saw the death of around 4,000 Scots, including the two commanders, the powerful noblemen the Earl of Douglas and the Earl of Buchan. Verneuil was described as 'a second Agincourt' and effectively ended the Scottish military adventure in France.

Individual Scotsmen, however, elected to continue fighting, especially if the pay was good. Some mercenaries formed the royal corps of bodyguards known as the Garde Écossaise. Others made up a significant part of the army of Joan of Arc during her victory over the English at the Siege of Orléans. Joan's famous battle standard was made by a painter resident at Tours, one Hauves Poulnoir – or, as the folks back in Scotland knew him, Hamish Power. On a darker note, a Scottish officer by the name of Spalding was one of the procurers of victims for Joan of Arc's former companion-in-arms, the aristocratic Gilles de Rais, who murdered more than a hundred children.

CLAN V. CLAN

For centuries, Scots fought against their traditional enemies – themselves. Perhaps as many Scots were killed in clan battles as they were in organised warfare – because although the numbers involved in each engagement were usually smaller, clan battles took place that much more frequently. Indeed, many major conflicts – from the Wars of Independence to the Jacobite Rebellions – typically had a major if often forgotten clan dimension. Robert the Bruce, for example, had to defeat Clan MacDougall before he could even think of taking on the English.

In 1396 an unusual clan battle took place – unusual because it was organised more like a combination of gladiator combat and football match, with spectators betting on the outcome. Two 'teams' of thirty men apiece formed up on an open space in Perth, and went at each other with swords, spears, axes and bows and arrows. Crowds thronged the barriers and grandstands. Within minutes one side was down to just eleven men still breathing, while the other had only one man standing – and he promptly swam across the River Tay to safety.

This 'Battle of the Clans' remains a deeply puzzling episode. We don't know why there was a dispute in the first place, and although we know the winners were Clan Chattan, the real identity of the losers – supposedly 'Clan Kay' – has never been established. A heavily fictionalised account appears in Sir Walter Scott's novel *The Fair Maid of Perth*.

Another trial by combat took place near Wick in Caithness (Highland) around 1478. Clan Gunn and Clan Keith had been at daggers-drawn for years, so they decided to resolve the issue with a 'Battle of Champions'. Twelve mounted men on each side were appointed – but the Keiths arrived with two men per horse, and despite heavy losses, their numerical superiority won the day.

On the 500th anniversary of the battle the chiefs of the respective clans travelled to the site and signed a Bond of Covenant and Friendship between the Keiths and the Gunns.

Supposedly, churches offered a sanctuary from the bloodletting of the clan feuds. Not so. In 1490 members of Clans Drummond and Campbell trapped a number of Clan Murray in the church at Ochtertyre in Perthshire – and set fire to the thatched church, burning them alive. A similar church-burning massacre occurred at Trumpan on Skye in the 1530s (the MacDonalds were the burners, the MacLeods the victims). Sometime between 1485 and 1487 several hundred women, children and old men of Clan MacKenzie were shut up in the church at Contin (Ross-shire, Highland) and burned alive by the MacDonalds. And in 1603 another party of MacDonalds burned another set of MacKenzies in a different church, this one at Kilchrist in the Black Isle (Highland).

Most clan battles perforce took place on land. But for the Islemen, naval warfare was also the norm. In the early 1480s the massed galleys of John of Islay, the Lord of the Isles, clashed with those of his son, Angus Og Macdonald, in a sea battle so sanguinary that the location, off Mull, is still known as Bloody Bay. Angus was the victor, but his forces were so depleted by the conflict that the Lordship of the Isles was soon eclipsed as a military force, and the kings of Scotland gained the ascendancy.

THE WARS OF MARY, QUEEN OF SCOTS

The last conflicts between the independent nations of Scotland and England centred on a little girl born in Edinburgh Castle in 1542.

At the age of six days, Princess Mary became Mary, Queen of Scots – her father, James V, having died of an illness possibly connected to his defeat by the English at the Battle of Solway Moss.

The immediate question arose: whoever eventually married the infant queen would become King of Scotland, a nation with a number of useful ports, a good trade base, and – most importantly – a highly strategic location. Both England and France wanted in. Henry VIII of England pressed the suit of his young son Edward. A treaty was signed. But when out-manoeuvred by the pro-French party in Scotland, Henry moved from carrot to stick: a series of punitive raids that saw the destruction of Edinburgh and several Lowland locations, a gambit known as the 'War of the Rough Wooing'.

The plan did not work; at the age of five, Mary was secretly sent to France, where, thirteen years later, she married the Dauphin, who soon became King Francis II of France. A French-Scottish confederacy was on the cards. When Francis died young, however, Mary was now superfluous to the ambitions of the French court and in 1561 she was shipped off to Scotland, where she landed to find herself in a country in the midst of its greatest revolution yet – the Reformation.

Even stranger, the Port of Leith had just witnessed a scene that demonstrated just how much the world had changed. A Catholic French garrison had been besieged by a Scottish Protestant army. Unable to dislodge the French, the Scots sent for assistance to the only Protestants within reach – the English. Just a few years before, England and Scotland had been at war, with the French assisting the Scots. Now the English were fighting with the Scots to expel the French. The Anglo-Scottish wars were over: the wars of religion were about to begin.

Catholic Mary became the cat's-paw of Protestant and Catholic factions. By 1567 she was faced with a full-scale rebellion and was forced to abdicate in favour of her 1-year-old son James VI. The following year she raised an army and tried to reclaim the throne. Defeated at the Battle of Langside in Glasgow, Mary fled to England. Scotland descended into six years of civil war between her supporters and opponents. Edinburgh Castle was besieged for two years, only being taken by the Protestant faction when English artillery arrived. The castle at Dumbarton changed hands, Rutherglen Castle in Glasgow was destroyed, Dumfriesshire saw raids, and there were battles and sieges across Aberdeenshire and the north.

After more than eighteen years as a discomforting presence in various English castle prisons, Mary was found guilty of plotting against Elizabeth I of England, and executed. The question of her guilt remains inconclusive to this day.

FOR KING AND COVENANT

By comparison with popular interest in Mary, Queen of Scots and the Jacobites, the Covenanter Wars are almost forgotten, despite the fact that the number of people killed far exceeded the casualties in all the other conflicts put together. There are three reasons for this – firstly, the battles and political allegiances of the Covenanter era are deeply confusing. Secondly, this was a war of religious principles, with little of the romance of Bonnie Prince Charlie and his ilk about it. And thirdly, to a modern mind the fanatical, intolerant Covenanters are hardly what you might call sympathetic.

Seventeenth-century Presbyterianism was a rather dour and avowedly anti-Catholic form of Protestantism that was at the time unique to Scotland. The official religion abjured bishops and any signs of what it called 'Papistry'. The Anglican Church in England, however, was run by bishops. When Charles I attempted to impose Anglican worship on Scotland in 1637, many Presbyterians signed what was called the National Covenant, dedicated to preserving the 'true reformed religion' from any sign of Anglicanism (which Covenanters saw as being merely watered-down Catholicism).

The following decades saw a whirlwind of religiously inspired warfare. The Covenanters defeated the forces of Charles I in Scotland. They sent an army to Ireland to protect Scottish Protestants from Irish Catholic rebels. They intervened in the English Civil War, assuring the victory of Cromwell's forces over Charles I. Then in 1644 civil war broke out between the Covenanters and Scottish supporters of the king, with many of the latter being Episcopalians (Anglicans) or Catholics. When Cromwell's English Parliament refused to make England a Presbyterian state, the disgruntled hard line Covenanters invaded England whilst at the same time promising aid to the exiled Charles II if he swore, when he regained the throne, to make Presbyterianism the state religion of the whole of Britain.

Throughout this period, Scottish domestic and foreign policy was dictated by little more than religious fanaticism.

Cromwell, the Covenanters' erstwhile ally, defeated the Covenanter invasion and occupied Lowland Scotland for almost a decade. The Covenanters were sidelined. Then in 1662 Charles II, now in power, thumbed his nose at the Covenanters and broke all the promises he had made to them when he needed their help. The Episcopal/Anglican church, with its hated bishops, was imposed on Scotland once again.

The once-triumphant Covenanters were now the victims of widespread state persecution. Armed rebellion broke out. Battles were fought. Covenanters were imprisoned and executed, many without trial. Some were cut down in the fields as they attempted to escape, or even after having surrendered. The period became known as the Killing Times. Throughout all the horrors – and horrors there were many – the Covenanters retained an iron grip on their faith, and the graves of many Covenanting 'martyrs' can be found throughout Lowland Scotland.

During this period Scotland also invented the concentration camp. In 1679, large numbers of Covenanter prisoners were incarcerated within a roofless enclosure in Edinburgh's Greyfriars graveyard. Denied adequate food, water and blankets, many died of exposure or starvation during the winter.

The last execution of a Covenanter took place in 1688. Perhaps 18,000 died for their beliefs in the main persecution period from 1661 to 1680, while thousands more perished in the earlier battles – a series of military interventions that had a profound if now hardly remembered role in the English Civil War.

THE JACOBITE REBELLIONS

Without Bonnie Prince Charlie and his ilk, one suspects that the Scottish tourist industry might as well just pack up and go home. Jacobite nostalgia is widespread. It is also curiously selective.

Most people think there were two Jacobite Rebellions one in 1715, and the other – the more famous, because of Bonnie Prince Charlie and the Battle of Culloden – in 1745. In fact the first major rebellion took place in 1689, and there was also a short-lived invasion in 1719.

The word Jacobite comes from Jacobus, the Latin word for James, and is named for James II of England and VII of Scotland, who was deposed in 1688 for his Catholicism, a bloodless coup known (by the Protestant victors) as the Glorious Revolution.

James II and VII was a Stuart, the family that (Oliver Cromwell's Commonwealth republic aside) had been on the throne of England since 1603, and had ruled Scotland from as far back as 1371. More than 300 years of being top dog was not easily shrugged off, even if James had been deposed, not by an outsider, but by his own daughter Mary, and her husband, William of Orange.

James II and VII prompted the Rebellion of 1689. When it failed, he remained in exile in France. In 1715 his son, James Edward Stuart, raised the second Rebellion from exile. It too failed. In 1745 Charles Edward Stuart, the grandson of James II & VII, raised the final rebellion from exile. Bonnie Prince Charlie's daring gamble nearly succeeded. But after the Battle of Culloden in 1746, the ambitions of three generations of Stuarts to reclaim the throne were dashed for ever.

Perhaps understandably, the Jacobite adventure is often seen entirely from a Scottish perspective. But Scotland was merely the board where the game was played out – the real player in the game was France. As a European Catholic superpower, France found in James II and VII (and subsequently his son and grandson) a convenient means of confounding England's ambitions. If the Jacobites came to power with French help, England and Scotland would be vassal states of France, Catholic confederates in the fight against the Protestant nations of northern Europe. And if the Jacobites did not succeed, then at least they tied up some of the enemy's resources. For France, it was a win-win situation.

1689 AND ALL THAT

The 1689 Rebellion is marked by the brilliant victory of the Jacobites over a Government army at the Battle of Killiecrankie in Perth & Kinross. The architect of the triumph, John Graham of Claverhouse, known to some as 'Bonnie Dundee', was, like Nelson at Trafalgar, killed at the very moment of his victory. Without his inspired generalship, the Jacobite advance faltered.

Far more important than Killiecrankie, although far less celebrated, was the Battle of Dunkeld, where a small force of fanatical Covenanters defeated a much larger Jacobite army flush with the success of Killiecrankie. This was another example where religion shaped the politics of warfare. The Covenanters had been mercilessly persecuted by the state for their beliefs; but the Jacobites were principally Catholics, and so the anti-Catholic Covenanter zealots now fought with the Government. As a consequence of the Battle of Dunkeld and the political horse-trading that followed, the Episcopal/Anglican religion ceased to be the official faith of Scotland: Presbyterianism was back.

To this day, the Church of England is Anglican; but the Church of Scotland is Presbyterian. This state of affairs is directly attributable to the Battle of Dunkeld in 1689.

THE '15 AND ALL THAT

The Rebellion of 1715 was marked by poor planning and extreme ineptitude on both sides. Typical of the state of affairs was the Battle of Sheriffmuir in Stirling District, where neither side could tell whether they had won or not. By the time James Edward Stuart took ship from France and landed in Peterhead (Aberdeenshire), the Rebellion was almost already defeated. He swiftly departed.

In 1718 a proposed Jacobite invasion sponsored by Sweden came to nothing. The following year a Spanish-financed expedition also fizzled out, although a tiny force landed on the west coast. With no proper planning or support, the Jacobites were not surprisingly eliminated at just one minor battle, in Glen Shiel (Lochalsh, Highland).

The next two decades were rife with invasion plans, plots and counter-plots. All came to nought.

THE '45 AND ALL THAT

In 1744 the French planned to invade Britain and place Charles Edward Stuart on the throne. Their fleet never left Dunkirk. Bitterly disappointed, in 1745 Charles decided to effect what was basically a one-man invasion.

It is easy to see why Bonnie Prince Charlie has captured the imagination of generations. The previous Jacobite rebellions were lacklustre and inconclusive affairs, largely led by individuals who appeared to be unable to organise a drunken evening in a brewery. But the 24 year old had dash, verve and glamour. He was able to do what his father and grandfather could not: he could inspire. With precious little in the way of money or support, Charles and a small band of companions set sail from France and landed on the Hebridean island of Eriskay. By the normal run of things, the entire rash adventure should have ended as just a minor footnote in history. As it was, it provoked the most serious challenge to the British state until the world wars of the twentieth century.

Charles mobilised the clans loyal to the Stuart cause and marched south. The results were astonishing. Edinburgh fell without any fuss. The Jacobites defeated a Government army at the Battle of Prestopans in East Lothian. Outmanoeuvring two other armies, the Jacobites marched into England. It seemed possible they could take London.

In one of the most-debated turning points in history, the Jacobites reached Derby, but then elected to return back to Scotland. This then effectively became a long retreat, dogged by Government forces all the way.

In January 1746 the Battle of Falkirk brought the two armies together, with the Jacobites only realising they had won when they surveyed the battlefield the following morning. Although they had won some breathing space, the retreat north continued.

Fought in appalling weather conditions, and laced with confusion and chaos, with no clear narrative or heroic exploits, Falkirk is the forgotten battle of the '45. Unlike Culloden, with its visitor centre and the accompanying dark glamour of defeat, at Falkirk you'd be hard-pressed to even find the site of the battlefield.

Sir John Cope, the commander of the losing Government army at Prestonpans, had learned to his cost just how good the Jacobite 'rabble' really was. As the loser, Cope was scapegoated by the Government and fired. Cope, however, knew that his replacement, Lieutenant-General Henry Hawley, like other Government generals, would seriously underestimate the Jacobite capabilities. He therefore cunningly placed a bet against his own side – gambling that Hawley would lose his first battle. Not surprisingly, he got good odds. After the Battle of Falkirk, Cope gleefully collected his winnings – £10,000, around £850,000 in today's terms.

CULLODEN

On 16 April 1746 the last pitched battle on British soil was fought on a desolate, waterlogged moor 5 miles from Inverness. In less than an hour, the Jacobite army was wiped out.

Some versions of the battle, even today, claim that this was a clash between England and Scotland, ignoring the fact that around a third of the Government army was made up of Scots. Once again, there was a clan dimension to the conflict, with traditional clan enemies facing up to each other, the war allowing the legitimate exercise of clan hatred.

The victorious Government army murdered the Jacobite wounded and prisoners, and unleashed a reign of terror across the Highlands, slaughtering and burning without caring whether the victims were Jacobites, Government supporters or merely indifferent to the whole affair. These atrocities left an indelible mark on Highland culture.

Charles Edward Stuart went on the run, helped by many who courageously risked their lives to help him. No one ever claimed the bounty of about £2.5 million (in modern terms) that would have been awarded had they betrayed Charles to the Government. After many celebrated adventures and close shaves, he took ship to France, never to return. The Jacobite adventure came to an ignominious end.

The romantic aura surrounding the young and handsome prince tends to obscure some unpalatable facts. For a start, he was a man whose beliefs came from a vanished age. Britain had slowly been evolving towards a constitutional monarchy, where Parliament limited the powers of the king. Charles, however, believed in the Divine Right of Kings – if he had come to power, Britain would have slipped back into the tyranny of an absolute monarchy. By 1789, the ghastly attitudes of the absolute monarchy in France led directly to the execution of the king and the formation of a republic. If Bonnie Prince Charlie had become King Charles III, then perhaps eighteenth-century Britain would have had its own equivalent of the French Revolution.

After his escape from Scotland, Charles Edward Stuart became a political irrelevancy. He continued to live in disappointed exile, and died in 1788, having spent his last years as a much-mocked, fat, ugly, drunken wife-beater. Not surprisingly, it's the handsome golden boy of romantic legend that people tend to celebrate.

THAT'S RADICAL

The late eighteenth and early nineteenth centuries saw the rise of movements centred on social justice and the reform of the political system. In the 1790s only one man in a hundred in Scotland had the right to vote, a franchise so narrow that it made the notoriously restricted English voting system seem liberal by comparison. Perhaps not surprisingly, the authorities were not inclined to be lenient with these 'radical' ideas.

When a peaceful convention dedicated to voting reform met in Edinburgh in 1793, the leaders were arrested and transported to Botany Bay in Australia. Only one of these 'Scottish martyrs' made it back to Britain alive, although a second ended up living in France, safe from the British authorities because a cannonball had disfigured his face so badly that he was no longer recognisable.

During the so-called 'Radical War' of 1820, some 60,000 impoverished weavers and other artisans went on strike across Lowland Scotland. Small unco-ordinated clusters of strikers started making impromptu edged weapons. Amongst the gentry, there was widespread fear that a second French Revolution was about to erupt. It all fizzled out when soldiers apprehended a group of men marching on the Carron Ironworks in Falkirk, where they had hoped to acquire guns and cannon. Mass arrests and the presence of the army brought the unrest to an end, but not before the militia fired on a crowd in Greenock (Inverclyde), wounding ten people and killing an 8-year-old boy.

Twenty radicals were transported to the penal colonies in Australia, while three were sentenced to death, one in Glasgow and two in Stirling. In bizarre scenes reminiscent of earlier centuries, the trio were hanged – and then beheaded with an axe. The black-masked executioner then held up each head and proclaimed, 'This is the head of a traitor.'

Soon after the events of 1820, it became clear that the Radicals had been pushed into action by government spies in their ranks. Without these *agents provocateurs*, perhaps nothing would have happened. In 1835 all the convicted Radicals were given an absolute pardon.

After many years of agitation, the Reform Act of 1832 started to make the political landscape a bit more democratic. Glasgow, for example, long the largest city in Scotland, finally acquired its first Member of Parliament.

THE EMPIRE STATE

By the late nineteenth century the British Empire was at its zenith. And at the sharp end could often be found Scottish regiments, whose kilts and bagpipes became an icon of imperial warfare, splashed across newspapers, magazines and 'boys' own' publications, never mind oil paintings, commemorative china and cigarette cards. From the Crimea and the Indian Mutiny to campaigns in the Sudan, Egypt, South Africa and Afghanistan, Scottish soldiers were often in the thick of the fighting.

In 1854, at Balaclava in the Crimea, 650 men of the Highland Brigade, a hundred of them invalids, formed into just two lines in the face of a charge by an overwhelming force of Russian cavalry. Three volleys later the Russians were in retreat, leading to the famous description of 'the thin red streak tipped with a line of steel', which is usually misquoted as 'the thin red line'.

For their bravery during the siege of Lucknow during the Indian Mutiny (1857), no less than eight soldiers of one Highland Unit, the 78th, were awarded Victoria Crosses. Elsewhere during the Mutiny, the 42nd also won eight VCs, and the 93rd seven. The sight of kilted soldiers and the sound of bagpipes often unnerved the enemy even before a shot had been fired.

THE FIRST WORLD WAR – THOSE WHO SERVED

No one really knows the full extent of casualties during the carnage of the First World War – which is why memorials to the 'Unknown Soldier' are so widespread. Probably at least 100,000 Scots died in the conflict, representing about 10 per cent of the adult male population of the time.

Widespread poverty in the industrial cities of Scotland meant that many men regarded joining up as a valid financial option. Scots eventually made up 15 per cent of the British armed forces, although the country had only 10 per cent of the British population.

Sixty-seven Scots were awarded the Victoria Cross in the First World War.

More than one third of these VCs – twenty-four in total – were awarded posthumously.

Most of the Victoria Crosses were of course awarded for actions in the trenches of the Western Front in France and Belgium. But some were for bravery in war zones much further afield.

Perthshire-born John Craig won his VC in Egypt. He was a 2nd Lieutenant with The Royal Scots Fusiliers.

From the same regiment came Private David Lauder of Airdrie (North Lanarkshire), who had his foot blown off in Gallipoli, Turkey. Petty Officer George Samson, from Carnoustie in Angus, also received a Victoria Cross for his bravery under fire during the same campaign.

Lieutenant-Colonel Sir Reginald Graham of the Argyll & Sutherland Highlanders received his VC for an action in Mesopotamia (now Iraq); Graham was from Cardross in Argyll & Bute. Another member of the Mesopotamian campaign, Private Charles Melvin from Kirriemuir in Angus, won a VC while fighting with the Black Watch.

Henry Ritchie of Edinburgh, captain of the battleship HMS *Goliath*, won his Victoria Cross for a naval action at Dar-es-Salaam, Tanzania.

Joseph Watt, the Chief Skipper of HM Drifter *Gowanlea*, set his small lightly armed vessel against the might of an Austrian cruiser in the Strait of Otranto, between Italy and Albania; it must have been like a wasp attacking a buffalo. He later saved the lives of the crews of other drifters attacked by the big warship. When he returned to his native Aberdeenshire, he never once discussed his wartime experiences and his Victoria Cross, not even with his nearest and dearest.

Archibald Smith, from Cults in Aberdeenshire, was the master of the merchant ship SS *Otaki* when it was engaged by the heavily-armed German raider SMS *Möwe* in mid-Atlantic. The *Otaki* had just one gun. Nevertheless the two ships engaged in battle and the *Möwe* was damaged before it sank the British vessel. Smith went down with his ship. As a merchant seaman and not a naval officer he was not entitled to a Victoria Cross, but so great was his gallantry that he was posthumously promoted to the rank of Lieutenant in the Royal Navy Reserve, thus allowing the VC to be awarded.

The Scottish National War Memorial is in Edinburgh Castle. Initially erected to honour the dead of the First World War, it now commemorates all Scots killed in action in all wars since 1914. At the time of writing, this figure is in excess of 206,000. Reading the Roll of Honour, it is nigh on impossible not to be moved to tears.

THE FIRST WORLD WAR – THE WAR AT HOME

Scotland's industrial might brought it a vital role in providing war materiel. Glasgow in particular was a powerhouse of armaments manufacture and other vital supplies.

Cordite was so essential as a propellant for shells that a cordite factory 9 miles long was built at Gretna in Dumfries & Galloway. The four main production units were interlinked by a narrow-gauge railway network that in total stretched for 125 miles. Two townships, complete with laundries, bakeries and police stations, were also constructed to house the 30,000 people working at what was described as 'the greatest munitions factory on earth'. Its immense output – up to 800 tons of shells a week – was vital to the eventual Allied victory.

The gigantic factory has long been demolished, but is commemorated at the Devil's Porridge Exhibition between Gretna and Annan. The 'Devil's Porridge' was the mix of nitro-glycerine and gun cotton used to make cordite.

Although aircraft had been used on the Western Front since the early days of the war, the traditional military mind still saw these new-fangled contraptions as good for little more than observation, and maybe the dropping of the occasional bomb by hand. An ambitious plan to prove that aeroplanes could attack targets on the ground led to the construction of Britain's first aerial gunnery school at Loch Doon, west of Dalmellington in East Ayrshire. Although the concept was sound, the outcome was poor, as the new airfield was so badly sited on marshy ground that it was almost useless. After a vast expenditure and an enormous engineering effort, which included the construction of a light railway, a shed for seaplanes, and all the facilities of a small town, the entire project was scrapped as being a waste of money. Barely anything remains today.

THE FIRST WORLD WAR –
THE WAR AT SEA

The Bass Rock lighthouse off the east coast was switched off during the war so as to not accidentally assist German U-boats. British naval vessels had to send a message to the lighthouse if they wanted it switched on. In October 1915 one such message was lost in transmission, and so the cruiser HMS *Argyll* ended up running aground. All the crew were rescued, the heavy guns were salvaged – and then the ship was deliberately blown up. Her propellers were recovered from the seabed in 1970.

In 1917 submarine *K13* sank to the bottom of the Gareloch (Argyll & Bute). After fifty-seven hours trapped underwater, forty-eight of the eighty men aboard were rescued. Look closely at the memorial in Faslane Cemetery and its surrounding headstones, and you will see that the ensemble is in the shape of a submarine, complete with conning tower.

After the ceasefire in October 1918, seventy vessels of the German Navy, from destroyers to battleships, were interned at the great harbour of Scapa Flow in Orkney. The following year the mighty fleet was scuttled by the few German sailors still on board. Although many were subsequently raised and recycled for scrap, seven of the warships still lie on the seabed – the cruisers *Brummer*, *Dresden*, *Karlsruhe* and *Köln*, and the battleships *König*, *Kronprinz Wilhelm* and *Markgraf*.

THE SECOND WORLD WAR

Part of the road system in the Orkney Islands owes its construction to a German U-boat. In October 1939 the submarine penetrated the Royal Navy anchorage of Scapa Flow and sank the battleship HMS *Royal Oak*. As a consequence the defences were improved and causeways built between several of the islands, thus blocking the eastern approaches to Scapa Flow. These 'Churchill Barriers,' as the causeways were known, now provide road access between the Orkney Mainland and the islands of Burray and South Ronaldsay.

The first air raid in Britain took place on 16 October 1939, over the Firth of Forth and Edinburgh. Two warships were badly damaged and ten sailors lost their lives. The only casualties in Edinburgh were several people injured – not by the Luftwaffe, but from the bullets fired by the pursuing Spitfires.

Scotland's topography was essential to the British war effort. The firths provided shelter for Royal Navy ships. Glasgow's position on the Clyde, facing North America, made it one of the pre-eminent supply ports for both raw materials and military forces, especially in the run-up to D-Day. Arctic Convoys to Russia left from the Clyde, from Oban (Argyll & Bute) and, most frequently, from Loch Ewe in Wester Ross (Highland). Also in the far north-west, the remote lochs around Kylesku provided the training waters for a flotilla of midget submarines, including those that put the German battleship *Tirpitz* out of action in a daring raid inside Trondheim harbour in Norway.

The 'Shetland Bus' was the name given to a secret operation that brought British and Norwegian agents between Nazi-occupied Norway and the Shetland Islands. The extremely hazardous operation was, for the first two years of its life, conducted entirely by ordinary small fishing boats.

Scotland was used as a base for many European combatants fighting the Nazis who had occupied their homelands. The largest group were probably the Poles, who manned coastal defences in Fife and had bases through Perth & Kinross. The huge Cross of Lorraine above Greenock in Inverclyde is a memorial to the Free French who fought in the Battle of the Atlantic.

A full-size mock-up of part of Hitler's Atlantic Wall, used for training assault troops in preparation for D-Day, still stands on Sheriffmuir above Dunblane in Stirling District, the ruins bearing the scars caused by live ammunition and explosives.

In October 1943 a Scottish pigeon saved the lives of a bomber crew. The Beaufort, having been hit by enemy fire, ditched in the North Sea. Unable to radio their position, the crew released Winkie – one of the aircraft-carried carrier pigeons for such emergencies – and the bird flew 120 miles to arrive, exhausted and covered in oil, at her home in Broughty Ferry (Angus). The owner immediately informed RAF Leuchars in Fife, and a successful rescue mission brought the men home. Winkie became the first recipient of the PDSA Dickin Medal, the 'animals' Victoria Cross'. She is on display in Dundee's McManus Art Gallery and Museum.

One of the strangest episodes of the Second World War took place on 10 May 1941, when Rudolf Hess, Deputy Führer of the Nazi party, flew his Messerschmitt Bf 100 to Scotland, parachuted out at Eaglesham (East Renfrewshire), and stated he wished to negotiate a peace deal. The true nature of Hess' unauthorised, personal mission has intrigued historians and conspiracy theorists ever since, especially after Hess died under mysterious circumstances in 1987, and some people have suggested that the man who spent a lifetime in a Berlin prison was in fact an imposter.

The Fairy Flag at Dunvegan Castle on Skye is a medieval banner that was reputed by Clan MacLeod to have magical properties. MacLeods serving in the RAF carried photographs of the Fairy Flag as protection against sudden death.

Sir Robert Watson-Watt, the man who invented radar and hence helped the RAF win the Battle of Britain, was born in Brechin (Angus), where a statue showing him holding a Spitfire and a radar tower commemorates his achievements.

A magnificent bronze statue of three tough-looking soldiers stands near Spean Bridge (Lochaber, Highland). It commemorates the Commandos, the special operations force whose training ground from 1942 to 1945 was at nearby Achnacarry, where incredibly demanding training took place amidst arduous mountain territory. This training included exercises using live ammunition and explosives (which saw some men lose their lives, and caused damage to Achnacarry Castle).

By the end of the Second World War some 25,000 men had been trained at Achnacarry, including the US Army Rangers, and volunteers from many countries of occupied Europe. A further training area, the Commando Mountain and Snow Warfare training camp, operated in the Cairngorm Mountains from Braemar in Aberdeenshire.

In December 1944 the largest escape from a prisoner-of-war camp in Britain saw ninety-seven Italians tunnel out of Camp 112 at Doonfoot near Ayr (South Ayrshire). The escape was less a bid for freedom and more an attempt to air grievances about conditions in the camp. Most of the escapees simply hung about waiting to be captured, while four of the more determined individuals managed to evade custody for a few days.

One of the most chilling episodes of the Second World War took place on the small uninhabited island of Gruinard, between Ullapool and Gairloch in the north-west Highlands. Up until 1990 signs around the edge of the island still read: 'This island is Government property under experiment. The ground is contaminated with anthrax and dangerous. Landing is prohibited.'

It was 1942. Britain was experimenting with ways to attack Germany using biological warfare. Eighty sheep were tethered on Gruinard and small 'anthrax bombs' were exploded nearby. Within three days the sheep started to die. The scientists conducting the tests realised that anthrax was useless as a weapon, as any German city or land exposed to the spores would be uninhabitable for generations. As it was, it took almost fifty years and a clean-up campaign costing more than half a million pounds before Gruinard was declared safe, and the warning signs were taken down. A flock of sheep now graze untroubled on the island.

A 16mm film of the Gruinard experiments remained classified and secret until 1997. It can now be seen on YouTube.

FIGHTING MEN

If you've ever enjoyed the exploits of C.S. Forester's fictional naval hero Horatio Hornblower, or Russell Crowe playing Captain Jack Aubrey in the film *Master and Commander*, then meet their real-life inspiration: Thomas Cochrane. Born in Hamilton (South Lanarkshire) and raised in Culross (Fife), Cochrane became a daring and unconventional warship captain during the Napoleonic Wars, earning the title of 'the Sea Wolf'. Slung out of the Royal Navy on a false charge of fraud, Cochrane, a natural Radical, promptly led naval battles promoting the independence of Chile and Peru from Spain, Brazil from Portugal, and Greece from the Ottoman Empire. He later returned to naval service in Britain.

Five vessels of the Chilean Navy have been named after Cochrane. The most recent, *Almirante Cochrane*, is the former Royal Navy Type 23 frigate, HMS *Norfolk*.

If Thomas Cochrane's biography hints at serial or divided loyalties, they were nothing compared to those of a certain seaman born near Kirkcudbright (Dumfries & Galloway) in 1733. After a successful career as a merchant sailor on various British ships, John Paul switched allegiance to the revolutionaries of the newly created United States of America, where he changed his name to John Paul Jones. He is often characterised as the founder of the United States Navy, although British perspectives at the time saw him as little more than a pirate.

Having been the first captain to hoist the US ensign on a naval vessel, Jones attacked various British vessels from the east coast of Canada to the Irish Sea. A brief incursion onto the Dumfriesshire coast near Kirkcudbright in 1778 was followed a year later by a circumnavigation of the whole of Scotland, which created 'invasion panics', especially on the east coast. At the Battle of Flamborough Head off Yorkshire, Jones defeated the Royal Navy warship HMS *Serapis*, a feat which sealed his reputation and formed one of the key moments in the American Revolutionary War.

John Paul Jones was, it appears, not an easy man to like, and he fell out with his crews, his superiors and fellow captains. In 1782, fed up with America, he signed up with the Russian navy in its fight against the Ottoman Turks. Again embittered by his experiences, he retired to France, where he died without obtaining another command. In 1906 Jones' remains were shipped from Paris to the USA, where the destroyer USS *John Paul Jones* is the latest in a line of warships named after America's 'first naval hero'. His birthplace, now the John Paul Jones Cottage Museum, can be visited at Kirkbean, south-west of Dumfries.

During the raid on St Mary's Isle near Kirkcudbright in 1778, Jones' crew plundered the silver service of the Countess of Selkirk. Jones later purchased the silver and returned it to the countess with a letter of apology.

Unlike the majority of British Army officers, Sir Colin Campbell came from a very humble background – his father was a Glasgow carpenter. His real surname was MacIver, but he enlisted under his uncle's name. At the Battle of the Alma in 1854, the first major conflict of the Crimean War, Campbell led the vastly outnumbered Highland Brigade up a steep slope against the right wing of the Russian army. Although the assault force was only two men deep – and therefore could have easily been broken – so determined and disciplined were the Scots that the Russians on the heights fled, and the battle was won.

During the famous 'thin red line' defence at the later Battle of Balaclava, Campbell shouted, 'There is no retreat from here, men! You must die where you stand!' There was no retreat. Both events are tribute to the high regard with which the Highland soldiers regarded Campbell – if he was leading, they would follow him anywhere, confident of victory.

5

TRANSPORTS OF DELIGHT: FROM HORSE TO HOVERCRAFT

ROAD TRANSPORT
BEFORE THE MOTOR CAR

Scotland's first stagecoach service opened between Edinburgh and Leith in 1610. It failed, largely because of the poor quality of the roads. Road conditions saw off many subsequent attempts to run stagecoaches, and it wasn't until the early 1700s that stagecoaches finally became part of the usual traffic scene in Lowland Scotland.

The Highlands were of course different. Before 1725 there was only one road in the whole of the Highlands that was able to take wheeled traffic.

Between 1725 and 1733 General Wade built 250 miles of engineered roads and some forty stone bridges in the Highlands, and from 1743 onwards even more miles of Highland road were added by Wade's successor General Caulfeild. These military roads were designed to provide quick movements of troops between castles and barracks in the event of a repeat of the 1715 Jacobite Rebellion. When the 1745 Rebellion broke out, the high-quality roads provided speedy access for Government soldiers and Jacobites alike.

Military roads aside, no one wanted to bear the cost of building (and maintaining) a road which strangers could travel upon for free. As a result, most roads in Scotland remained in an abysmal state. In 1780, for example, the good people of Stewarton in East Ayrshire petitioned for improvements in their area, stating that the roads, 'in the winter season and wet weather even for travelling on horseback [are] impassable.'

From 1766 onwards, several Acts of Parliament authorised the setting up of turnpike trusts, which then constructed good-quality toll roads, where travellers were stopped at tollbars and tollgates and charged for using the highway. Pedestrians and churchgoers were exempt from the tolls, as were ministers of religion and soldiers on the march, but everyone travelling by carriage, wagon, horse or mule had to pay up, as did drovers of livestock. In 1774 a top-of-the-range coach drawn by six horses was charged eight shillings, while a single horseman had to pay half a shilling, and cattle were charged at one-and-a-half shillings for every twenty beasts. Bridges had entirely different sets of charges, and usually made everyone – including pedestrians – cough up.

In theory the tolls would disappear once the cost of building the road had been met. In practice, of course, this didn't happen, and travellers constantly grumbled about the cost of tolls. Many tried to cut across open land just before the tollbar to avoid the charge, but as more and more wasteland became enclosed and developed, this became a chancy business – sometimes trespassers found themselves looking down the barrel of a landowner's gun.

The unpopularity of the tolls brought forth protests, even riots. In 1869, for example, disgruntled locals at Dunkeld (Perth & Kinross) used gunpowder to blow up a nearby folly in protest at the Duke of Atholl continuing to charge excessive tolls on Dunkeld Bridge.

The coming of the railways spelled the end of the turnpike trusts, many of which saw their income drop to the point of bankruptcy. Tollbars were dismantled throughout the country. In 1888 all main roads became the responsibility of local councils, and the last tolls disappeared.

Many modern roads follow the routes of former turnpikes. Thus wherever you travel in Scotland, you are likely to be – at least part of the time – taking a route that would have been familiar to people 200 years ago.

A little south of Ayr, at Brown Carrick Hill, is an otherwise nondescript minor road that would appear to be of little interest – but it was here that the world's first experimental 'macadamised' surface was laid in the 1780s. The mile-long stretch just happens to pass the driveway of Sauchrie House, the South Ayrshire home of John Loudon McAdam, whose name lives on in the now-universal tarmac.

McAdam and his Scottish contemporary, Thomas Telford, built roads in different ways. In the early twentieth century, before the original roads had been remade, motorists used to say that you could tell a McAdam road from a Telford road by the number of times you needed to change gear (Telford being the winner in this comparison).

ROAD NAMES

Dere Street was the principal Roman road in south-east Scotland. The modern A68 from Carter Bar runs along part of the route.

In the Middle Ages the route of Dere Street was known as the Via Regia, the 'Royal Way', as it linked the capital, Edinburgh, with the powerful abbeys of the Scottish Borders – Jedburgh, Kelso, Dryburgh and Melrose.

The Royal Mile in Edinburgh is so called because it runs from Edinburgh Castle to the queen's residence at Holyrood Palace.

There is a Duke's Road and Duke's Pass near Aberfoyle in Stirling District. Both owe their name to the Duke of Montrose, whose nineteenth-century toll road across his estate became freely open to the public in 1931 when the Forestry Commission purchased the land. And a very scenic drive it is too.

The Serpentine Road on the Isle of Bute is well named – fourteen hairpin bends ascend a steep hill in about a third of a mile. The record time for cycling it is a lung-busting 1 minute and 57 seconds.

The B880 across central Arran is known as The String – because from the sea it does indeed look like a piece of string laid over the mountains.

Calum's Road on the island of Raasay is named for Malcolm (Calum) MacLeod, who single-handedly constructed the road over ten years – with only a second-hand book on road building as his guide.

Toot Corner is the name of a sharp bend near Abbey St Bathans, in the former county of Berwickshire (Scottish Borders). An old road sign at each end of the bend reads 'TOOT'.

The most famous road name in Scotland is Rest and be Thankful, which is the moniker of the spot where the A83 passes over the Arrochar Alps in Argyll & Bute. Once you've finished the long slow climb from Glen Croe, you'll understand why eighteenth-century travellers were thankful for the rest.

In 2013 the town of Keith in Moray finally acceded to demands from the emergency services and gave official names to no less than fifty-four old lanes, none of which had ever featured in street directories.

THE ROADS YESTERDAY

Scotland's first private motorist was Thomas Elliot of Linton in the Scottish Borders, who purchased a French Panhard-Levassor car in 1895.

In 1896 George Johnston was fined for driving his car in Glasgow's St Enoch's Square. At the time, cars were legally regarded as steam locomotives.

Scotland had three early home-grown car manufacturers. Arrol-Johnston started in Paisley in the late 1890s and later moved to Dumfries. Although at one point it was the fifth largest car manufacturer in Britain, the company folded in 1929. Argyll operated out of Glasgow and Alexandria in West Dunbartonshire, but collapsed in 1914. Albion (of the Borders and then Glasgow) ceased car production in 1912, preferring to concentrate on the less fickle lorry market. It survived the ups and downs of the twentieth century and was later absorbed into British Leyland.

THE ROADS TODAY

In 2011, 186 people died in fatal accidents on Scotland's roads, a reduction of 41 per cent compared with a decade earlier.

The most dangerous year for road users was 1969, when 892 people were killed on Scotland's roads. The numbers have been progressively declining ever since.

The title 'the most dangerous road in Scotland' has been applied to a number of notorious motoring black spots, based on accident and/or fatality statistics. Candidates have included: the A99 from Latheron to Wick (Caithness/Highland); the A708 Moffat to Selkirk (Scottish Borders); the A937 Montrose to Laurencekirk (Aberdeenshire); the A81 towards Callander (Stirling District); the A70 Balerno to Carnwath (Edinburgh/South Lanarkshire); the A809 at Glasgow; and stretches of the A9 in Perth & Kinross and Highland.

With a length of 273 miles, the A9 between Polmont (Falkirk District) and Scrabster Harbour, Thurso (Caithness/Highland) is the longest road in Scotland. The 'great road to the north' used to be longer, but the section starting in Edinburgh has been renamed or replaced by other roads.

Many roads in the north – including the A9 and other main routes – have snow gates, which are closed when conditions become too severe for driving. Something of an annual ritual surrounds the moment when Radio Scotland announces the first road closure of the winter, which is always the B974 Cairn O'Mount road from Fettercairn to Banchory in Aberdeenshire's Cairngorms.

In 1965 there were reports from the Cairngorms of a 'phantom car', a black 1932 Austin Seven spotted travelling mysteriously on impossibly snowbound roads. This was in fact the conveyance used by four students from Loughborough College on a skiing holiday at Glenshee. Whenever confronted with a snowdrift, the quartet simply carried the car over the snow to the next driveable stretch of road.

The island of Easdale (Argyll) has a population of about sixty, but no roads, no streetlights and no cars.

MOTORWAYS

Scotland's first motorway was the M8, linking Glasgow and Edinburgh. The earliest sections, the Townhead Interchange in Glasgow and the

Renfrew Bypass, opened in 1968. The M8 continues to be extended and improved but the overall structure was complete in 1980.

The M8 Kingston Bridge over the River Clyde in central Glasgow is often claimed to be the busiest road in Europe.

The first motorway service station in Scotland was Harthill on the M8, opened in 1978.

CYCLING

The first pedal-driven bicycle was invented by the splendidly named Kirkpatrick Macmillan, from Kier in Dumfries & Galloway. It was probably in use by 1839, and the sight of the twenty-something blacksmith careering about on his two-wheel velocipede earned him the nickname 'Daft Pate'. Macmillan did not take out a patent and went largely unrecognised as the inventor of the self-propelled bicycle. A plaque commemorating him reads: 'He builded better than he knew'.

The replica of another early Scottish bicycle, built in 1845, can be seen in the Glasgow Museum of Transport.

The Royal Albert Cycling Club in Larkhall (South Lanarkshire) was officially founded in 1887, but its history may stretch as far back as 1872, making it one of the earliest cycling clubs in Britain.

In the 1880s the Scottish Cyclists' Union started installing a new form of road signage, hazard-based rather than direction-based. A typical one read: 'CYCLISTS this hill is DANGEROUS.'

The North Sea Cycle Route runs around all of the eight countries bordering the North Sea. 772 miles of the 3,700-mile total are in Scotland.

RAILWAYS

The title for 'the first Scottish railway' is disputed. A good candidate is the Kilmarnock and Troon Railway, which opened in 1812. Unlike most railways, where the flanges of the wheels are guided by the upright edges of the rails, the Ayrshire operation was a plateway, where ordinary wheels ran on flat metal plates. All trains were pulled

by horses, and ordinary horse-drawn carts also used the plateway, which served more as an 'iron road' than a proper railway.

Like most early railways, the K&T was conceived as a way of moving coal. Soon, however, passengers were realising the benefits of this new form of transport, and were travelling in open straw-filled trucks.

The 10-mile journey between Kilmarnock and Troon cost one shilling (about £2 in modern currency) and took around two hours, much faster than travel by road. The modern age of high-speed transport had arrived.

From around 1817 the K&T tried using a steam locomotive instead of horses, but the experiment was not a success, as the plates could not take the weight. The first successful locomotive-driven railway in Scotland was the Monkland & Kirkintilloch Railway, which had started transporting coal from the Lanarkshire collieries to the Forth & Clyde Canal in 1826, and switched from horses five years later – its two small locomotives could reach a top speed of 5mph. The same year, 1831, and with much more fanfare, the Garnkirk & Glasgow Railway opened a passenger and goods service from north-west Glasgow to the city centre. Scottish transport had entered 'the age of steam'.

From the 1830s onwards railways proliferated at a bewildering rate. Competition for goods and passengers was cut-throat, and the owners of rival transport systems (such as stagecoaches and canals) tried every means possible to delay or disrupt the new-fangled trains and their annoying tendency to travel as fast as 20 or even 30mph.

In 1845 surveyors working on a proposed line at Glen Falloch, south of Crianlarich (Stirling District), found themselves under physical attack by supporters of a rival railway company. Such encounters were not uncommon during the period of 'railway fever'.

The massive expansion of railway building provided manual work for thousands of men, many of them from Ireland and England. These navvies could sometimes be a handful. In 1845, on the anniversary of the Jacobite Rebellion in 1745, anti-English remarks were fired at some English railway navvies drinking in a pub in Dunblane (Stirling District). A fight broke out, and then the Englishmen marched to the top of a nearby hill, surrounded the Gathering Stone, a symbol of the 1715 Jacobite Rebellion – and blew it up with dynamite.

As with the rest of the UK, Scotland's railways were severely cut in the 1960s. Many lines closed forever, including the Carlisle to Edinburgh route, which left the Scottish Borders as the only region of Britain without a train service. The major line from Dumfries to the port of Stranraer was also shut, as were Aberdeen to Ballater and Dyce to Fraserburgh and Peterhead, and several lines in Fife, Perthshire, Angus and the Highlands.

The Borders town of Hawick, 56 miles from Edinburgh and 42 miles from Carlisle, is the largest Scottish town so far from a railway station.

The 50-mile section between Lockerbie and Carstairs in the Scottish Borders is the longest stretch of railway line in the UK without an intermediate station.

Having been opened in 1849, Laurencekirk station in Aberdeenshire closed in 1968, saving British Rail a few thousand pounds. The station reopened in 2009, the process costing £3 million. In the first year of its new operation, twice as many passengers used Laurencekirk than had been originally projected.

According to Constance Fredereka Gordon-Cumming, who wrote *In the Hebrides* in 1883, the locals at Kyle of Lochalsh (Highland) knew that the railway would be coming to their tiny port some three decades before it finally arrived. The knowledge had been granted in a series of prophetic visions. Several people with the second-sight saw, 'a huge dark coach with fiery lamps — they could see no horses; only a great glare of flames and sparks, and it rushed past them at a place where there was no road, and vanished among the mountains.'

The most lethal train crash in British history saw around 226 deaths at Quintinshill, Dumfries & Galloway, in 1915. Some of the fire-consumed bodies were never recovered. The exact number of fatalities could not be determined because many of the dead were soldiers whose regimental roll list was destroyed in the disaster.

The West Highland Line between Glasgow and Mallaig has twice been voted the most scenic railway line in the world (2009 and 2010). A steam-driven train, *The Jacobite*, runs special trips in the summer months.

The line includes one of the least-used stations in Scotland: Falls of Cruachan, a request-only (and daylight-only) stop visited by around 200 hillwalkers a year.

Corrour on the West Highland Line is the highest station in the UK. The nearest public road is 10 miles away, which means Corrour shares the title of the most remote railway station in Britain with the equally lonely Altnabreac in Caithness (Highland). It is unclear why Altnabreac is even there, as there were no dwellings in the area when it was built. Even now, the request-stop railway station is only one of four buildings in the area.

Dunrobin Castle station in Sutherland (Highland) was originally built as a private halt for the immensely wealthy Dukes of Sutherland, whose extraordinary chateau-like confection of a castle is now a major tourist attraction. Trains on the Far North Line between Inverness and Thurso/Wick stop at the once-exclusive station in summer.

There are currently seven heritage railways operating in Scotland. The ones at Alford Valley (Aberdeenshire), Almond Valley (West Lothian) and Leadhills & Wanlockhead (South Lanarkshire) are all small narrow gauge railways, while the enthusiasts at Bo'ness & Kinneil (Falkirk District), Brechin (Angus), Royal Deeside (Aberdeenshire) and Strathspey (Highland) have either preserved or reinstated the original full-width tracks. The longest distance you can go on a steam train is at Strathspey – 10 miles.

The longest rail journey in Britain without changing trains starts at Aberdeen and ends at Penzance in Cornwall thirteen and a half hours later.

TRAMS

There were once eighteen tramway systems in Scotland, covering not just the major cities but smaller urban areas such as Ayr, Perth, and Kirkcaldy in Fife. All have now vanished, the last being in Glasgow, which closed in 1962. A new tram network is underway in Edinburgh.

BUSES

The Scottish Vintage Bus Centre near Dunfermline in Fife houses Scotland's largest collection of preserved and under-restoration buses.

Their earliest motor vehicle dates from 1922, although they also have a horse-drawn Edinburgh street tram from 1885.

The most unusual bus shelter in Britain is on the island of Unst in Shetland. Situated near the village of Baltasound, it is kitted out as a fully decorated living room, complete with television set and seats.

FERRIES

With so many firths, sea lochs and inhabited islands, Scotland is, you might say, 'away with the ferries'. There are currently over sixty scheduled ferry services within Scotland, ranging from small passenger boats to sea-going ships.

The busiest route is across the mouth of the Firth of Clyde between Gourock and Dunoon, with more than 1.3 million passengers a year.

The shortest ferry routes in Scotland are Kylerhea-Glenelg (Skye/Lochalsh) and Easdale-Ellenabeich (Argyll), both of which typically take around five minutes. The longest ferry journey, by contrast, is between Aberdeen and Lerwick in Shetland, lasting twelve hours.

Kylerhea on the Isle of Skye has the only turntable ferry in the UK. The turntable that rotates the six-car platform is entirely operated by hand.

One of the most famous road signs in Scotland is 'Strome Ferry (No ferry)'. The sign can be seen on the way to the village of Stromeferry on Loch Carron, in Wester Ross (Highland). The ferry across the loch was withdrawn in 1970. 'Strome Ferry (No ferry)' is a running joke in Iain Banks' novel *Complicity*.

HOVERCRAFT

Back in the early 1960s futurists peered into their crystal balls and predicted that hovercrafts would be the transport of choice for the late twentieth century. It didn't quite work out that way, but a few pioneers took up the challenge – especially in Scotland.

In 1962 the *Denny D2 Hoverbus* made its maiden voyage from its home at Dumbarton to Oban, then through the Caledonian Canal to Inverness, and down the east coast of England, where thereafter it operated sightseeing tours on the River Thames. The venture failed when the Denny shipyard at Dumbarton went bust.

On 16 June 1965 Clyde Hover Ferries commenced the UK's first daily hovercraft service, operating principally on the commuter route between Dunoon on the Cowal peninsula and Gourock with its rail link to Glasgow, and to the Clyde holiday resorts of Rothesay, Wemyss Bay, Millport and Largs.

The hovercraft simply came ashore on the beaches. The 'terminal' at Largs, for example, was just a stretch of pebbly beach with a rope as a paltry barrier, and a caravan for a booking office.

The service was real 'seat of the pants' stuff, with the company and pilots learning as they went along. The quality of the operation was probably not enhanced by the flamboyant owner's rather eccentric behaviour – such as interrupting the schedule to give day trips for his friends, or filling the hovercraft with the sheep he kept on the island of Little Cumbrae.

The hovercraft base was, ludicrously, located at Tarbert on Loch Fyne, many miles from the Clyde market. Engineering problems, bad weather and high costs all contributed to the service lasting no more than a summer.

The next attempt to run a hovercraft ferry in the Firth of Clyde came in 1970, when the Caledonian Steam Packet Company (the forerunner of today's ferry giant Caledonian Macbrayne) ran a service between Largs, Millport, Dunoon and Rothesay.

The scooshin' cushin', as it was known locally, was registered not as a boat but as an aircraft, and journeys were logged as 'flights'. The craft was certainly fast, but the noise and uncomfortable bouncing, combined with the high cost and persistent engineering problems doomed the operation, and after two unsatisfactory seasons the craft was sold back to the manufacturers in 1972.

In 2007 and 2008 hovercraft ferries were trialled on the Forth and Clyde respectively. Despite initial enthusiasm, the ventures went no further. To the disappointment of those who fancy arriving at their destination by sliding up a beach on a cushion of air, there are currently no commercial hovercraft operating in Scotland.

FLIGHT

You could argue that John Damian de Falcuis was the first Flying Scotsman as, bedecked with wings made from chicken feathers, it was he who launched himself into the air from the ramparts of Stirling Castle in 1507. The argument would fail, however, on two counts: one, that Damian was Italian; and two, that his flight consisted entirely of falling into a dunghill below the castle and breaking his leg. Back to the drawing board, Signor de Falcuis.

Scotland's – and indeed Britain's – first man in the air was actually James Tytler, whose balloon rose 350ft above Edinburgh in 1784. The pioneering but failure-prone Tytler never achieved the recognition he deserved, and other, more glamorous aeronauts took his place in the hearts and minds of the fickle public.

Hot air balloons rise because the air inside their envelope is hotter than the air in the atmosphere outside. The dream, however, was for heavier-than-air human flight. The first such experiment in Britain took place in 1895 at Cardross (Argyll & Bute), overlooking the Firth of Clyde. Percy Pilcher, a shipbuilding engineer and an assistant lecturer at Glasgow University, strapped himself into a primitive hang-glider called *The Bat*, faced a headwind, and rose 12ft into the air, remaining aloft for twenty seconds. Pilcher's second attempt pushed the height to 20ft, and the flight time to almost a minute. The age of the aeroplane was, rather falteringly, born.

The era of powered flight began on 17 December 1903, when American aviator Orville Wright famously flew his *Wright Flyer I* for 120ft at Kitty Hawk, North Carolina. There are hints that around the same time, or even before, Dundee-born Preston Watson flew a powered aircraft for a short distance at Errol (Perth & Kinross). A magazine article from 1957 claimed that agricultural workers had witnessed the first flights in the summer or autumn of 1903, several months before the Wright Brothers entered the history books. Watson was definitely flying by 1906 or late 1905, making him the genuine first Flying Scot; but the Errol farmworkers' claims have never been authenticated, and Watson himself died in the First World War while serving with the Royal Naval Air Service, so whether he actually made the world's first powered flight will never be known.

In July 1914 Norwegian Tryggve Gran, pioneer aviator and Polar explorer (he found the bodies of Captain Scott's ill-fated South Pole

expedition team in 1912), became the first person to fly across the North Sea. The hazardous 410-mile crossing across tempestuous waters started at Cruden Bay in Aberdeenshire. At take-off, Gran's tiny monoplane only just missed hitting the overhead electrical cables powering the trams that served the Cruden Bay Hotel.

The first commercial airport in Scotland opened at Renfrew in 1933, when the site was still known as Moorpark Aerodrome. The initial scheduled flights were to Campbeltown in Argyll, with later additions to London's Croydon Aerodrome.

Renfrew Airport closed in 1966, the operations being transferred to the new Glasgow Airport at Abbotsinch, 2 miles away. Most of the old airport is now beneath the M8 motorway.

The Scottish Air Ambulance Service originated with an impromptu flight from Renfrew to Islay in 1933, to evacuate a fisherman close to death with acute peritonitis. With conventional travel times from the Highlands and Islands being so great, it became obvious that a speedy emergency service was required. The SAAS has subsequently saved the lives of a huge number of people, and is one of the glories of Scotland.

Scotland has the shortest scheduled flight in the world. The Loganair journey between Westray and Papa Westray in the Orkney Islands takes all of two minutes, including taxiing.

Barra Airport in the Western Isles is the only runway in the world where scheduled services land on the beach.

Mount Everest, 3 April 1933: two Scottish daredevils, Flight Lieutenant David Fowler McIntyre and Douglas Douglas-Hamilton, Marquis of Clydesdale, become the first pilots to fly over the highest mountain in the world. Pushed to the feat because American flyers had already 'bagged' the North and South Poles, the Scots achieve their aim under fearsomely dangerous conditions, only to learn that their cameras have failed. Strictly against orders, and in true *Boys' Own Adventure* style, the dashing fly-boys do the whole thing again on 19 April, and this time get the pictures. Twenty years later, Sir Edmund Hilary and Sherpa Tenzing used these same photographs as a guide when climbing Everest.

Scotland has the largest area of permanent restricted airspace in the UK. Whereas most other restricted airspaces are relatively small (for example, over nuclear power plants, high security prisons and Buckingham Palace), large swathes of the Highlands and the adjacent sea areas are restricted because of the high number of low-level military training flights that take place there.

With so many offshore oilrigs and windfarms in the North Sea, it's hardly surprising that Aberdeen has the busiest civilian heliport in the world.

6

FOOD & DRINK

SCOTTISH FOODS

Scottish shortbread is not a bread, but a sweet biscuit (or, if you are American, a cookie). The defining element of shortbread is the use of butter ('shortening') instead of vegetable fat. Other than that, it contains the standard biscuit ingredients of flour and sugar. Most Scottish shortbread is produced by Walkers Shortbread of Aberlour in Moray; Walkers is the largest food exporter in Scotland.

Supposedly, shortbread was invented by Mary, Queen of Scots, and if you believe that, you'll believe Robert Burns invented the haggis served at Burns Suppers. It is possible, however, that Mary (or more likely a cook in her employ) may have made certain refinements, such as the addition of caraway seeds.

Porridge is eaten across northern Europe, but is especially associated with Scotland. The reason for its popularity is that the Scottish climate, especially in the Highlands, is well-suited for growing oats. Rolled oats and oatmeal were therefore relatively cheap, and hence became the standard form of cereal carbohydrate for the majority of people.

'Real' Scots porridge is supposedly eaten with just water and salt; most people today, however, choose milk and sugar. Wimps.

The quintessential Scottish winter food is stovies – potatoes stewed ('stoved') with onions and corned or minced beef.

Smoked salmon and Loch Fyne oysters form part of the bounty of the Scottish water world, along with lobsters and langoustine. Indeed, visiting Scotland without sampling its seafood would be a culinary crime.

The walled orchard at the National Trust for Scotland Priorwood Garden at Melrose Abbey in the Scottish Borders cultivates many historic apple varieties, some dating from the Middle Ages – look out for Cowsnout, Foxwhelp, Catshead and Old Wife.

Depending on the nature of your supplier or restaurant, you can sometimes find pheasant, grouse or venison on the menu, while wild boar is farmed in a few places – not to mention ostrich. Despite the superabundance of bunnies in Scotland's soil, however, rabbit meat is rarely available.

Chicken tikka masala, Britain's favourite curry dish, was invented in Glasgow in the 1960s.

Haggis – basically offal mixed with oatmeal cooked in a sheep's stomach – may have originated as a way of keeping meat-based food fresh while travelling. The stomach would have acted as a combined Tupperware box and carry basket.

Haggis – especially on Burns night – is traditionally consumed with neeps and tatties (turnips and potatoes).

Haggis is the Marmite of meat dishes – you either love it or hate it.

Foods associated with specific locations include: Arbroath smokies (smoked haddock); Abernethy biscuits; Moffat toffee; Aberdeen butteries (savoury bread); Ayrshire bacon; Forfar bridies (a meat pastry); Dundee cake and Dundee marmalade; Selkirk bannock (flat bread); and the wonderfully-named Cullen skink (a thick soup based on smoked haddock).

Jethart Snails are made in the Borders town of Jedburgh (which is sometimes pronounced 'Jethart'). No molluscs are involved – the 'snails' are minty boiled sweets.

Scots is a creative, vigorous language, especially when it comes to food. Crappit heid ('stuffed head') is indeed stuffed fish head. Cabbie claw is another fish dish. A tattie scone is a potato scone. Clapshot is turnips and potatoes mashed with chives, while rumbledethumps is a 'leftovers' meal of cabbage, potato and onion.

Rumbledethumps is apparently the favourite food of former Prime Minister Gordon Brown, who was brought up in Fife. In 2009 he submitted a rumbledethumps recipe to a charity cookbook.

For dessert, you could try cranachan (cream, whisky, honey, oatmeal and raspberries), Atholl brose (oatmeal, honey and whisky), crowdie (cream cheese, usually eaten with oatcakes), black bun (pastry covered fruitcake), tipsy laird (trifle with whisky or Drambuie), or clootie dumpling (a heavy pudding, traditionally cooked in a cloth or 'cloot').

The Scottish sweet tooth is more commonly served by such 'traditional' mass-manufactured local goodies as Tunnocks Teacakes, Tunnocks Caramel Wafers, Lees Snowballs and Lees Macaroon Bars, all of which have been popular for decades.

Reports that the deep-fried Mars bar has joined the ranks of Scottish cuisine are not entirely exaggerated. Although they are rare today compared to their late 1990s heyday, the batter-coated chocolate bars can still occasionally be found – usually in takeaway establishments that also offer deep-fried pizzas.

In 1909 Ernest Suffling published *Epitaphia: Being a Collection of 1300 British Epitaphs Grave and Gay, Historical and Curious*, in which he claimed that on the Isle of Skye you could find the gravestone of a man whose epitaph stated he had died from eating a surfeit of scones. It is not clear if this epitaph really existed, or whether Mr Suffling was having us on.

WHISKY A-GO-GO

'Scotch Whisky' is a protected brand name. No whisky made outside Scotland can be called 'Scotch'.

In Scotland the word is always spelt 'whisky', with no 'e'. 'Whiskey' with an 'e' is a drink manufactured elsewhere, such as America, Japan or Ireland.

The word 'whisky' is derived from 'usky', the phonetic corruption of the Gaelic word *usquebaugh*, meaning 'water of life'.

'Water of life' in Latin reads as *aqua vitae*. And *aqua vitae* is on record as being distilled in Scotland as long ago as 1494; the process is probably much older.

Whisky was originally regarded as a medicine, and in 1505 its manufacture and sale was restricted to the medical guilds such as the barber-surgeons.

Whisky at its most basic is the distillation of malted barley. Malt was first taxed in the seventeenth century, and then the whisky product itself was taxed, often heavily. The next 150 years or so saw a smuggling war, in which small-scale distillers sought to evade paying any tax – or 'excise' – by any means possible. Stills became portable – able to be dismantled and hidden when the excisemen came calling – and entire communities, from sailors to men of the cloth, connived in keeping the location of untaxed whisky barrels secret.

On the Isle of Arran alone, there were thirty-two illicit stills operating in 1784, and fifty by 1797. By the 1820s, 14,000 illegal stills were being confiscated across the country every year – and yet more than half of the whisky in Scotland was still being sold and consumed under the tax radar.

Whisky smuggling came to an end with the Excise Act of 1823. For a fee, anyone could now buy a licence to produce and sell whisky legally. This legitimating of the producers opened up new markets, both domestic and international, and profits rocketed: the Scotch whisky industry was born.

The era of illicit distillation and smuggling has contributed many colourful tales to the folklore and folk history of Scotland, typically of the 'cunning Highlanders outwit the wicked tax collectors' variety, and several modern distilleries like to tell these stories in their visitor centres. What tends not to be recalled is the number of times excisemen were assaulted or murdered in the course of their duty.

Malt whisky is made only from malted barley, and by law must have been matured in a barrel for at least three years. A single malt is the product of a single distillery. Well-known single malts include The Glenlivet, Lagavulin, Laphroig, Glenfiddich and Glenmorangie.

Blended Scotch whisky is a mix of malt and grain whiskies from several different distilleries. Blends – which include such famous marques as Johnnie Walker, Dewar's, Chivas Regal and Cutty Sark – account for 90 per cent of Scotch whisky sales.

About 100 distilleries are currently in operation – many welcome visitors. One suspects that for a number of such guests, the highlight is not so much the tour of the production facilities, but the tasting at the end.

A number of distilleries have closed over the years, and their remaining stock will obviously never be replenished – so prices of their single malts rise year on year.

In February 2013 thousands of litres of bulk whisky were accidentally flushed down the drain at the Chivas Brothers bottling plant in Dumbarton. Fortunately the whisky did not reach any rivers and the waste water treatment plant contained the discharge.

John Dippie's Well in the Lammermuir Hills (East Lothian and Scottish Borders) has a notice attesting to its 'sweet' water. This is a kind of joke, as Mr Dippie, a gamekeeper, used to please his shooting party clients by 'sweetening' the water with whisky just before they arrived.

MADE FROM GIRDERS

Scotland's other national drink is Irn-Bru, a bright orange carbonated sweet soft drink, originally known as Iron Brew. Referring to its 'rusty' colour, one of its advertising campaigns claimed that it was 'made from girders'. It should be pointed out that Irn-Bru does not contain iron, nor is it brewed. And as for being made from girders, well ...

The drink has been produced in Scotland since 1901, and regularly outsells Coca-Cola in its home market.

In 2013 limited-edition Irn-Bru bottles appeared adorned with distinctly Scottish personal names – Senga, Fanny, Rab and Tam.

One of the things that many people 'know' about Irn-Bru is that it supposedly cures hangovers. In truth, any drink that combines water and carbohydrates will help relieve the morning-after dehydration caused by overindulgence.

THE SWALLEY

Long before whisky became the national drink, the Scots were quaffing French wine. Imports commenced in 1295, when France and Scotland formed an alliance based on mutual detest/fear of the English. Claret – red wine from Bordeaux – was known as the 'Bloodstream of the Auld Alliance'. For centuries Scottish merchants had trading privileges that allowed them to snap up the best stocks of claret before any other wine buyers. Scottish drinking vessels even took on French names. The jug known as a chopin was derived from *la chopine*, a French pint glass.

In the eighteenth century any Scottish urban dweller of refinement drank claret in preference to whisky, which was widely regarded as the tipple of yokels and yobs. Robert Burns once described whisky as 'a rascally liquor drunk by the rascally portion of society'.

After the Act of Union between England and Scotland in 1707, tax was imposed on claret by the English authorities. It therefore became a patriotic duty for many Scots to drink claret on which no tax had been paid. Claret smuggling became big business, with many grandees in Edinburgh and elsewhere turning a blind eye to the legal niceties of the trade.

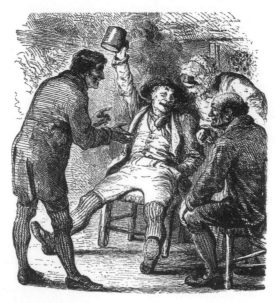

Wine is probably not what comes to mind when you picture Scotland's home-produced drinks – after all, the climate is hardly designed to provide the heat and sunlight required for vineyards to mature. But who needs grapes? In 1669 Highlanders were recorded making wine from the sap of the birch tree, and today several small producers offer very palatable wines made from berries, flowers and vegetables. Cairn O'Mohr Winery in Perth & Kinross, for example, uses everything from strawberries and gooseberries to oak and brambles, while the Orkney Wine Company has wines based on, among other products, rhubarb, rosehips, gorse flowers and carrots. Highland Wineries, based near Inverness, produces not only fruit wines but also mead, made from fermented honey.

Scotland's first vineyard in centuries was planted in 2011, in Fife. The viticulturist identified the primary threat to the grapes as being, not the weather, but the predations of the local roe deer.

Rùm, one of the Small Isles in the Inner Hebrides, was called 'Rhum' (pronounced 'Room'by some) for much of the twentieth century. This was because the former owner, Sir George Bullough, disliked the idea of being known as the 'Laird of Rum'.

Up until the 1970s Kirkintilloch in East Dunbartonshire was a 'dry' area, where no alcohol was available for sale (except to hotel guests) and there were no pubs or bars.

Alcohol abuse is estimated to cost the Scottish economy £2.25 billion a year.

TEA AND COFFEE

James Taylor from Aberdeenshire is known as 'the father of Ceylon tea'. From 1869, his revolutionary management of a tea estate in what is now Sri Lanka elevated tea from Ceylon over that of its traditional source, China, thus changing the drinking habits of first the British Empire, and then the world.

Sir Thomas Lipton was born in Glasgow and opened his first grocery shop there in 1871. Lipton's Tea was the first global tea brand – not only was the packaging the same everywhere in the world, but so was the quality and taste of the tea.

In a story which may or may not be true, English Breakfast Tea was supposedly created not in England, but north of the border, in Edinburgh, for a specific customer: a certain Queen Victoria. No such legend has come down to us about Scottish Breakfast Tea.

Scottish Blend, a tea specifically designed for Scottish water, was introduced in 1990 and is the second most popular brand in the country, after Typhoo.

Camp Coffee, a convenience drink made from a mix of coffee essence and chicory, was first produced in Glasgow in 1876 as a way for the armies of the British Empire to quickly brew coffee on the go.

After five years of small-scale local operations, fair trade coffee was first commercially distributed in Scotland in 1984. Fair trade coffee is now universally available, along with hundreds of other fair trade products, and Scotland achieved Fair Trade Nation status in 2013.

The most remote cuppa on the mainland can be enjoyed at the Ozone Café at Cape Wrath, the most north-westerly point of Scotland. There is no public road access, and after getting off the ferry across the Kyle of Durness the only way to get to the café is to take the café's minibus – or walk the 11 miles. In late December 2010 the co-owner of the café took a trip to Durness to buy a Christmas turkey – and was stranded by snow for two weeks.

7

CULTURE

SCOTTISH LITERATURE – THE EARLY DAYS

The earliest-known example of literature from Scotland, a long battle lament known as 'The Gododdin', was written in Old Welsh in the early seventh century by the bard Aneirin, who was based at what is now Edinburgh.

The Life of St Columba, a hagiography of the great saint, was written in Latin during the later seventh century by Adomnán, 9th Abbot of Iona. It is one of the most important documents of the European Dark Ages, and is still widely available. Those reading *The Life* expecting a conventional Christian worldview may be surprised, however, by both the very large number of incidents relating to magic and the supernatural found within the pages, and the way Columba is portrayed as a kind of cross between a sorcerer-druid and a politician-priest.

Adomnán's book, by the way, is the source for the oft-repeated story that St Columba confronted the Loch Ness Monster. For the record, the event – whatever it was – took place not in Loch Ness but the River Ness that leads into the loch from Inverness.

The Ruthwell Cross, a magnificent Anglo-Saxon stone cross at Ruthwell in Dumfries & Galloway, contains not just an inscription in Latin, but – very unusually – another in Scandinavian runes. The runes spell out part of an early Christian poem known as the 'Dream of the Rood', one of the very first works in Old English.

'Flytings' were long 'insult poems' written by poets patronised by the sixteen-century Scottish court. A flyting was a kind of upscale slanging match where the purpose was to be as creatively insulting as possible. In 'The Flyting of Montgomery and Polwart' (1580), for example, the author Alexander Montgomery claimed that his rival Patrick Hume of Polwarth ('Polwart') had an ape for a mother, a demon for a father, and was raised by a coven of witches. In some ways flytings were the precursor of the cruder 'insult' genre of modern rap music, where calling 'yo' Mama' an ape would be regarded as relatively mild.

In the seventeenth century Sir John Scot of Scotstarvit Tower in Fife wrote his political memoirs, *Scot of Scotstarvit's Staggering State of the Scots Statesmen, for one hundred Years, viz. from 1550 to 1650*, which was so libellous that it was only published after everyone he mocked in it was long dead.

LIBRARIES

The oldest free lending library in Scotland can still be found at Innerpeffray in Perth & Kinross. Founded about 1680, its books were available for free because the 3rd Lord Madertie, who funded the project, believed that this would benefit both scholars and local people alike. 'The Borrowers' Register' dates from 1747 and gives the names, addresses and occupations of the local people who borrowed books – and thus has become a treasure trove for genealogists and family history researchers.

The first subscription library in Britain was founded in Leadhills (South Lanarkshire) in 1741. All the founding members were miners except the village schoolmaster and the church minister, and the first purchases concentrated on religion and history. The library's revolutionary idea – that ordinary working men could educate themselves by reading books held in common and available for a small annual fee – had a huge impact. In 1756 the second British subscription library opened in the neighbouring mining village of Wanlockhead, and Westerkirk followed in 1792. The historic Leadhills library is open on weekends in summer.

RABBIE BURNS

As the national poet of Scotland, Robert Burns has naturally been eulogised, canonised, mythologised and, at times, sanitised. None of

this has detracted from his brilliance and his enduring legacy, which continues to inspire both writers and ordinary Scots to this day.

Like William Shakespeare in England, everything concerned with Burns' life and work remains of abiding interest. Burns came from a humble background in Ayrshire, growing up with the hard manual labour of farming. He began to write poetry at the age of 15.

Like many ambitious young men of the period, Burns was convinced the only way he could rise out of his dire financial situation was to emigrate to Jamaica. The voyage was called off when his first collection, *Poems, chiefly in the Scottish dialect*, became an unexpected success. All 612 copies sold out in the first month. It was 1786, and farmer Rabbie was about to take the Scottish literary world by storm. Soon, he was being lionised in Edinburgh society.

Burns' poetry is often characterised by themes of solidarity, fairness, equality, liberalism and even proto-Socialism. You wonder what this humanitarian would have made of working on a slave plantation.

By 1787 the 'Heaven-taught ploughman' had rocketed to fame and was widely regarded as the national bard. So, like any hardworking author, he went out and promoted his work. His tours of the Borders, the Highlands, Aberdeenshire and Stirlingshire were largely commercial in nature, but they also allowed him to collect traditional ballads and folk songs. Some of his finest work appeared in the six volumes of *The Scots Musical Museum*.

Again, like many authors, Burns' cultural success was not matched by an equivalent financial reward. He tried to return to farming, and then worked for the unpopular Excise (tax gatherers).

The years of pitiless farm labour took their toll of Burns' health. Prematurely aged, he died in Dumfries in 1796, at the age of just 37.

In 2009 STV (Scottish Television) conducted a viewers' poll to find who was regarded as the greatest Scot of all time. Burns won hands down.

Burns wrote the words for one of the most-sung songs in the world: the New Year anthem 'Auld Lang Syne'. Which, loosely translated from Scots, means roughly 'in remembrance of old times'.

His song 'Scots Wha Hae', with its patriotic tub-thumping, was the unofficial national anthem of Scotland for almost 200 years, and is the official party song of the Scottish National Party.

In 1965 World Heavyweight Champion boxer Muhammad Ali (then Cassius Clay) visited the Burns Country in Ayrshire and quipped in typical rhyming style: 'They told me his work was very, very neat, So I replied: 'But who did he ever beat?''

The 25 January, the anniversary of Burns' birth, is the night when thousands of Burns Suppers take place across Scotland and across the world – a tradition that dates back to 1802, just a few years after Burns' death. The highlight is the parade of the haggis – often accompanied by a piper – followed by the recitation of Burns' poem 'Address to a Haggis'. Oh, and everyone sings 'Auld Lang Syne'. All accompanied by lashings of whisky.

Probably the best-known piece of Scottish supernaturalism is Burns' 1791 narrative poem 'Tam O'Shanter', which is read aloud at Burns Suppers. Tam, having been drinking late, is passing Alloway Kirk (which is still there in South Ayrshire) when he sees witches and warlocks having a knees-up, the host of the dread party being the Devil himself. Tam draws attention to himself when he shouts in

approval at the appearance of an attractive semi-naked witch, and he only just escapes the subsequent hot pursuit by reaching the sanctuary of Alloway Bridge – the witches, as tradition demands, cannot cross running water, but the closest witch manages to pull out the tail of Tam's horse Meg just as he reaches safety.

INTO THE FANTASTIQUE

Scotland has a rich history of writing that explores what we now regard as the genres of fantasy, science fiction, ghost stories, horror and the supernatural – what the French call the *fantastique*.

One of the great obscure mysteries of the Middle Ages revolves around the enigma known as Thomas the Rhymer. On the one hand we have a man, historically recorded as Thomas Learmonth, a landowner from Ercildoune (now Earlston) in Berwickshire, Scottish Borders. Learmonth was also known as Thomas Rymour (Rhymer), although we don't know why. On the other hand we have a ballad, 'Thomas the Rhymer,' also thirteenth century in date, which tells how Thomas seduces (or is seduced by) the Queen of Elfland, and returns from a seven-year stint in Fairyland with the gift of prophecy. Thirdly, we have numerous prophecies ascribed to Thomas the Rhymer that were widely circulated throughout medieval Scotland but were not written down until the early 1600s. Finally, we have the well-known ballad 'Tam Lin,' which tells a similar tale of fairy seduction/abduction, only this time with the Fairy Queen being defeated by Tam's lover, a young human woman. Many writers have tried to work out the connections between Thomas the man, Thomas/Tam the ballad figure, and Thomas the prophet – and nobody can come to any solid conclusions.

Here's an entirely arbitrary list of ten excellent Scottish works of the *fantastique*:

The Strange Case of Dr Jekyll and Mr Hyde (1886) by Robert Louis Stevenson. If you haven't read it, do so now.

Lilith (1895) by George MacDonald, from Huntly in Aberdeenshire. MacDonald wrote several excellent fantasy novels; *Lilith*, with its haunted library and parallel universe, is the darkest, and his best.

The Lost World (1912) by Sir Arthur Conan Doyle, from Edinburgh. Yes, we know he created Sherlock Holmes, but with this novel Doyle also invented the 'dinosaurs live in modern times' genre, which later gave birth to both *King Kong* and *Jurassic Park*.

A Voyage to Arcturus (1920) by David Lindsay, who grew up in Jedburgh in the Scottish Borders. An extraordinary work delving into the meaning of life, with the central character departing from a deserted Scottish observatory and voyaging through several planets, each representing a different philosophical system.

The Haunted Woman (1922), also by David Lindsay. A hallucinatory ghost story set in a house that can access other dimensions.

Travel Light (1952), by Edinburgh's Naomi Mitchison, a droll, subversive sort-of fairy tale, which nowadays reads like a proto-Terry Pratchett.

The Star Fraction (1995) by Ken MacLeod, also from Edinburgh. The future will feature Artificial Intelligence, anti-technology terrorists and libertarian political activists.

The Algebraist (2004) by Fife-born Iain M. Banks. Full-on, galaxy-spanning, planet-sized-weapons science fiction. Banks' hugely popular 'Culture' series of novels – of which this is not one – posit an optimistic view of interstellar humanity in the far future. In the Culture, money is a sign of poverty and people can enjoy long lifespans of almost total freedom. Note: when Banks wrote 'mainstream' novels he used the name Iain Banks; his science fiction works were marked by the addition of the middle initial 'M.'

Halfhead (2009) by Aberdeen's Stuart MacBride. A near-future thriller set in a ghastly Glasgow, with big guns, lobotomised criminal zombies and a half-dead serial killer.

Pandaemonium (2009) by Christopher Brookmyre, from Barrhead in East Renfrewshire. Featuring: a high school visit to an outdoor activity centre in the Highlands, a secret underground military base, and an apparent portal into Hell.

FACT V. FICTION

Fingal (also known as Fhionn, Fionn mac Cumhail and Finn MacCool) and his war band the Fianna or Fingalians are the Irish mythological equivalent of King Arthur and the Knights of the Round Table. The great Fingalian cycle of interrelated tales of heroism, love, betrayal, magic, monsters and battles travelled with Gaelic storytellers when the Scots first came over from Ireland, and were quickly adapted to the local geography – you can find 'Fingal' or 'Finn' placenames and legends everywhere in Scotland, especially in relation to ancient sites. In the 1760s James MacPherson published a series of epic poems that he claimed he had translated from original Scottish manuscripts written in third-century Gaelic by Fingal's son, the bard Ossian. They were an international sensation. Fans included Thomas Jefferson, Walter Scott and Napoleon Bonaparte, who carried the book on campaign with him.

The Ossian poems had a huge impact on the burgeoning Romantic Movement, and inspired paintings, literature and operas right across Europe. Prominent people named their children after characters in the poems. Estate owners in Scotland 'Ossianised' their landscapes, adding Romantic follies such as Ossian's Cave and Ossian's Hall near Dunkeld in Perth & Kinross. Scotland became more and more associated with a kind of mystical, ancient Celtic glamour that still shapes many people's perception of the country.

In reality, however, Ossian was a hoax, a fraud, a clever and convincing falsehood. James MacPherson made the whole thing up.

In the 1780s James Grant, an advocate from Edinburgh, wrote two books explaining how the languages of Greek and Latin were descended from Gaelic, as the ancient Roman and Greek civilisations had been founded by emigrants from Scotland. It is fair to say that, in holding this opinion, Mr Grant was in a minority of one.

The real-life model for the fictional castaway Robinson Crusoe was Alexander Selkirk, a rough, troublemaking sailor from Fife.

In 1704, at the age of 28, the quarrelsome roustabout was deliberately marooned on an uninhabited island far off the coast of Chile. He survived for four years and four months, eating wild vegetables, berries and the flesh of feral goats. Twice he had to hide from enemy Spanish ships – had he been captured, he would probably have been executed. Despite having achieved an almost Zen-like calm state of mind on the island, Selkirk, once he was rescued by a British ship, vigorously returned to a life of quasi-legal piracy and getting into fights. He died in 1721, from yellow fever on board a ship off the west coast of Africa, two years after a certain novel called *Robinson Crusoe* was published by the English writer Daniel Defoe.

Although Defoe set the tale of his castaway in the Caribbean, it was clearly based on Selkirk's Pacific adventure. *Robinson Crusoe* was an instant hit and has never been out of print, becoming one of the stories of world literature that everybody knows, even if they haven't read the book. Selkirk's island home, Más a Tierra, is now officially known as Robinson Crusoe Island, while a statue of Selkirk stands at 101 Main Street in the small fishing village of Lower Largo, marking the cottage where the world's most famous castaway was born.

Daniel Defoe is also behind the literary legend of our next real-life person, Rob Roy MacGregor (1671–1734). Defoe published *Highland Rogue* in 1723, while Rob Roy was still alive, the highly romanticised account creating the illusion of a Scottish Robin Hood. The fictionalisation continued in 1817 with Walter Scott's *Rob Roy*, the novel becoming not just wildly popular but the basis for a stage play that, reaching a wide audience, established Rob as a genuine Scottish folk hero.

Were it not for Defoe and Scott, Rob Roy – Jacobite, honest cattle dealer, dishonest cattle thief, swordsman, extortionist, jailbreaker, outlaw and duelist – would have been largely forgotten outside the Central Highlands. As it is, the fiction has colonised the landscape of Stirling District, and you can find two Rob Roy's Caves (at Loch Voil and Loch Lomond), Rob Roy's Putting Stone (Glen Dochart), Rob Roy's Prison (Rowardennan), Helen's Pool (Ledard – named after Rob's wife), and many other elements named not after the hard man's actual life but the fiction of Scott's novel. Rob's grave (genuine – but reusing a sword-carved medieval graveslab from a much earlier era) can be seen at Balquidder.

THE MAN WHO INVENTED SCOTLAND

Sir Walter Scott (1771–1832) was a literary colossus, being in his day one of the most-read authors in the world. His historical novels and poems virtually single-handedly created the idea of 'Romantic Scotland' – and also invented many elements which have become part of the 'true' history of Scotland, even though they are entirely fictional.

When Queen Victoria visited Glasgow in 1849 she asked to see the home of Bailie Nicol Jarvie, the merchant who gets amusingly caught up in unwanted adventures in Scott's *Rob Roy*. Jarvie was entirely fictional; nevertheless Her Majesty was shown an old house where Jarvie supposedly lived – which happened to be next to a pub glorying in the name of the 'Original Bailie Nicol Jarvie Tavern'.

In *A Legend of Montrose* (1819), Scott fictionalised an area near Portlethen in Aberdeenshire as 'the Moor of Drumthwacket'. One of the local landowners duly changed the name of his farm from Banchory Hillock to Drumthwacket.

Scott's influence went far beyond the cultural, extending into the economic. Both *Rob Roy* and *The Lady of the Lake* (1810) turned the hills of the Trossachs in Stirling District into a mass-market tourist hotspot, while United Distillers named a whisky after Roderick Dhu, the hero of *The Lady of the Lake*.

Walter Scott's apogee as the 'Inventor of Scotland' came in 1822 when he organised the visit to Edinburgh of King George IV, an event in which an entirely inauthentic 'Highland pageant' changed the face of Scottish so-called traditional dress. Highland tartan, formerly the clothing associated in the Lowland mind with rogues, cattle thieves, Gaelic-speaking Catholics, Jacobite armies and other undesirables, suddenly became de rigueur. Lowland gentlemen, assisted by some very inventive Edinburgh kilt suppliers – who knew a good business opportunity when they saw one – suddenly developed a (very distant) Highland ancestry. The king himself turned up in a tartan costume that ranked somewhere between the flamboyant and the kitsch.

The 'King's Jaunt' of 1822 turned the divided Scotland of the Lowlands and the Highlands into a unified Tartan Scotland, at least in perception. Overnight, the once-despised tartan and kilt became the national dress of the whole of Scotland, and this is now an integral part of Scottish identity. Lowland culture had nothing that could compete with the visual spectacle of the kilt, or the dazzle and panache of tartan. Whereas once kilts were the feared sign of the linguistically, culturally and geographically distant Highlanders, now, in a reverse colonisation, tartan erased Lowland culture: the kilt had won.

If you attend a wedding in the Lowlands and all the men are wearing kilts, thank Walter Scott. If you see Scottish fans in kilts at an international sporting event, thank Walter Scott. If the next kilted bagpiper you see has a Lowlands accent – thank Walter Scott.

When people in the media talk about producing a documentary where the subject matter has a Scottish twist, they say, 'Let's put a kilt on it.'

JOHN BUCHAN

For most people, being a soldier, diplomat, colonial administrator, magazine editor, publisher, Member of Parliament, lawyer, war correspondent for *The Times*, Lord High Commissioner of the Church of Scotland, Deputy Chairman of the Reuters News Agency, traveller in Africa and the Arctic, Director of Intelligence during the First World War and the Governor-General of Canada might be enough for one life. The prodigiously energetic John Buchan, however, also managed to fit in the writing of almost thirty novels, several collections of short stories and dozens of non-fiction works.

Buchan is best known for inventing the genre of the 'man on the run' spy thriller. Richard Hannay, the resourceful South African hero pursued across the Scottish Borders in *The Thirty-Nine Steps* (1915), is in the DNA of Ian Fleming's James Bond and the works of John Le Carré and Frederick Forsyth, as well as numerous thriller movies.

Secret agent Richard Hannay returned to have further adventures in *Greenmantle* (1916), *Mr Standfast* (1919), *The Three Hostages* (1924) and *The Island of Sheep* (1936). Buchan revealed that he based the character partly on Edmund Ironside, a multi-lingual army officer from Edinburgh who used disguises to spy on the German colonial forces in South-West Africa before the First World War.

John Buchan's range was astonishing. He wrote biographies of Sir Walter Scott, the Marquis of Montrose, General Gordon, Oliver Cromwell and the Roman emperors Julius Caesar and Augustus. He produced a twenty-four-volume history of the First World War, and also covered church history, poetry, Scottish history, travel and adventure literature, autobiography, politics and sport.

Although *The Thirty-Nine Steps* has never been out of print and has been successfully translated to film, you suspect that Hollywood isn't about to option some of the more obscure corners of Buchan's output, such as *The Law Relating to the Taxation of Foreign Income*.

Buchan was born in Perth and spent much of his early life in Fife, Glasgow and the Scottish Borders. There is an excellent John Buchan Museum in Peebles, which is on the 13-mile long John Buchan Way.

CRIME PAYS

The best-selling Scottish writer of our times is Ian Rankin, whose Edinburgh-set novels account for around 10 per cent of all crime fiction sales in the UK. In 2009 Nielson Bookscan listed the top 100 bestselling authors of the previous decade and Ian Rankin came in at #15, having sold (up to that date) 6,848,039 books worldwide. A fellow Edinburgh writer, Alexander McCall Smith, author of *The No. 1 Ladies' Detective Agency*, was at #17, his sales over the previous ten years numbering a mere 6,609,779 copies.

Both these giants have a long way to go to match Highland author Alistair McLean, whose thrillers such as *When Eight Bells Toll* have notched up more than 150 million sales in total, or Edinburgh's J.K. Rowling, whose *Harry Potter* books stand somewhere between 350 and 450 million copies sold.

As the case of Ian Rankin shows, crime fiction is one of the strengths of Scottish literature. Here, then, is an entirely arbitrary list of ten recent-ish novels from the dark depths of the Scottish criminal imagination:

Laidlaw (1977) by William McIlvanney: 'it was Friday night in Glasgow, the city of the stare.' Hard-boiled 'mean streets' detective fiction in the Raymond Chandler mode.

The Wasp Factory (1984) by Iain Banks. Hardly what you might call a conventional crime novel, this extraordinary work nevertheless manages to pack in three child murders, a returning psychopath, and enough unconventional weaponry to power a guerrilla war.

Death of a Gossip (1985), by Glasgow-born M.C. Beaton (Marion Chesney), is the debut of Police Constable Hamish Macbeth, the local bobby in a remote Highland village. Beguiling and charming, it is next to impossible to read without picturing the main character as actor Robert Carlyle, the star of BBC Scotland's wonderful hit TV series *Hamish Macbeth*.

The Mermaids Singing (1995) by Val McDermid, from Kirkcaldy in Fife, marks the first appearance of McDermid's recurring protagonist, crime profiler Dr Tony Hill. Bloody, brutal, brilliant.

In *Morvern Callar* (1995) by Alan Warner, from Connel in Argyll & Bute, Morvern wakes up one morning to find her boyfriend's corpse in the kitchen. What to do with his valuable unpublished novel ...?

Quite Ugly One Morning (1996) by Christopher Brookmyre. The debut of professional gadfly and journalist Jack Parlabane, scourge of the corrupt Establishment. Not for anyone offended by copious bodily fluids of all kinds.

Cold Granite (2005) is set in author Stuart MacBride's native Aberdeen, 'the Granite City'. Here be put-upon Detective Sergeant Logan Macrae, his potty-mouthed boss DI Roberta Steel, and a rather nasty child killer.

The Burry Man's Day (2006), a 1920s period piece set in author Catriona McPherson's native South Queensferry in Fife, has great fun with the town's still-extant folklore figure, the vegetation-covered Burry Man.

No Suspicious Circumstances (2007) by the Mulgray Twins from Edinburgh. Fancy a crime story in which the investigator's sidekick is a sniffer-cat called Gorgonzola? Then the 'cosy crime' series featuring Customs & Excise officer D.J. Smith is for you.

Natural Causes (2013) by James Oswald, from Fife. Detective Inspector Tony McLean can sense the palpable, murder-hungry evil beneath Edinburgh's civilized façade.

COMICS

Desperate Dan. Dennis the Menace. Korky the Cat. The Bash Street Kids. Lord Snooty. Minnie the Minx. These icons all had their genesis in Dundee, where the publisher D.C. Thomson can be said to have largely created British comics culture. *The Dandy* first appeared in 1937, and was selling 2 million copies a week in the 1950s. It ceased publication in 2012 due to lack of sales. *The Beano*, dating from 1938, is still going.

D.C. Thomson's other successes include two weekly comic strips, 'The Broons' and 'Oor Wullie', which have appeared in the *Sunday Post* newspaper since 1936, and remain wildly popular. Unlike the anarchic hijinks of *The Beano* and *The Dandy*, which have universal appeal, the newspaper strips present an insular and couthy view of Scottish working class life, complete with dialogue in dialect that can be a challenge to outsiders (for example, the Broons are actually the Brown family, 'Broon' being the pronunciation in Scots).

In complete contrast is another long-running product of the D.C. Thomson stable, *Commando Comics*, a still-thriving small-format title started in 1961 and filled with tales of derring-do and heroism, typically set in the First or Second World War. I have every confidence that many male readers of a certain age will have fond memories of reading *Commando* as a boy.

MUSIC

The bagpipes had long been regarded as a way to rouse men into battle, and so martially-minded clans always made sure they had a piper or two at hand. The MacCrimmons were the hereditary pipers for the MacLeods of Skye, and guarded their musical secrets carefully. On one occasion a girl learned a particular combination of finger notes, and was intending to pass them on to an outsider. The MacCrimmons knew they had to prevent their clan copyright from being breached, so they did the obvious thing – they cut the girl's fingers off.

Along with tartan dress, bagpipes were banned in the years following the Jacobite Rebellion of 1745–46.

The iconic Scottish bagpipes are strictly known as the Great Highland Bagpipes. Other bagpipes played in Scotland – but with far less visibility – are the Border pipes, the bellows-blown pipes, the smallpipes and the reel pipes.

Other traditional instruments include the tin whistle, clarsach (small harp) and fiddle.

The only time Elvis Presley set foot on British soil was on 3 March 1960, when the aircraft bringing him back from military service in Germany refueled at Prestwick Airport in South Ayrshire. The uniformed Elvis

was on the ground for just under two hours, and signed autographs for around 200 fans who had learned of the 'hush hush' visit through the airport staff grapevine.

A carbon-offset Future Forests tree plantation on the Isle of Skye is dedicated as a living memory of Joe Strummer, the leader of punk group The Clash.

FILMS – THE EARLY DAYS

Short films were projected in theatres in Edinburgh, Glasgow and Aberdeen as early as 1896, although it took some time for cinema to move away from being basically a fairground or music hall sideshow to becoming an entertainment in itself.

Many of the earliest films were what were called 'phantom rides', where the camera was placed at the front of a moving vehicle, giving the audience the thrill of apparently experiencing the journey for themselves. At least two of these phantom rides still exist – *Glasgow Trams* from 1902, which runs through the city's busy Argyle Street, and the self-explanatory *Railway Ride over the Tay*, dating from as early as 1897.

The Hippodrome in Bo'ness (Falkirk), which opened in March 1912, is Scotland's oldest surviving purpose-built cinema building. The oldest cinema still showing films is the Picture House in Campbeltown (Argyll), which opened in May 1913.

Other early surviving cinemas can be found in Glasgow (the 1913 Salon in Hillhead, now a restaurant) and in Edinburgh (the 1914 Cameo, still showing films in a stunningly decorated auditorium).

SCOTTISH 'HISTORY' ON SCREEN

Mary, Queen of Scots has proven to be an irresistible subject for filmmakers, starting around the birth of cinema with *The Execution of Mary Stuart*, an 18-second-long 'bloody history' piece made by Thomas Edison in 1895. This extraordinary short – which convinced viewers unused to special effects that they were seeing a real execution – is the earliest representation of 'Scotland' on film. Watch it on YouTube – the moment when, in full view, Mary's head is cleaved from her shoulders still has the capacity to shock.

Mary has been played on screen by: Fay Compton (*The Loves of Mary, Queen of Scots*, 1923); Katharine Hepburn (*Mary of Scotland*, 1936); Vanessa Redgrave (*Mary, Queen of Scots*, 1971); Vivian Pickles (*Elizabeth R*, BBC drama, 1971); Elizabeth Taylor (*The Mirror Crack'd*, 1980 – playing an actress playing Mary); Clémence Poésy (*Gunpowder, Treason & Plot*, BBC drama, 2004); Barbara Flynn (*Elizabeth I*, Channel 4 drama, 2005); and Samantha Morton (*Elizabeth: The Golden Age*, 2007). There will doubtless be many more.

There is also a weird Nazi version, *Das Herz der Königin* (*The Heart of the Queen*, 1940) which shows Mary as a 'proper' woman whose only crime has been to love, while her rival Elizabeth I of England is depicted as, frankly, a cold-hearted domineering bitch. The propaganda element is obvious.

Bonnie Prince Charlie, inevitably, is another Scottish film star. The eponymous 1923 version, partly filmed on location, is now sadly lost. *Bonnie Prince Charlie* (1948, with David Niven as the Young Pretender) includes a considerable number of locations from the west coast of Scotland. *Culloden* (1964) stands in contrast to the usual romanticised nonsense by being a stark portrayal of the reality of the battle, as if being filmed by a documentary film crew on the spot. Also of note is *Chasing the Deer* (1994), which attempts an historically accurate account of the 1745 Rebellion, and which was partly funded by 374 people who each invested £1,000 and who appear as extras in the film.

Rob Roy is yet another favourite. A silent film named after him was released in 1922, while *Rob Roy, the Highland Rogue* was a Disney production in 1953, and Liam Neeson brought rather more gravitas to the role in 1995's *Rob Roy*, with the added bonus of some terrific Scottish locations.

Braveheart (1995) is by far the most commercially successful of all films set in Scotland. Supposedly the story of the thirteenth-century Scottish national hero William Wallace, its exciting epic battle drama obscures the fact that almost everything in the film – from costumes and characters to names and dates – is historically inaccurate. To give just two examples: Wallace is shown having an affair with the wife of Edward II, Isabella of France – who was in reality just three years old at the time; and the title 'Braveheart' was not that of Wallace, but of Robert the Bruce, who specified that after his death his heart be taken into battle. Oh, and we can't forget that in the film the Battle of Stirling Bridge, Wallace's greatest triumph, does not actually feature the bridge that was so crucial to the victory.

In 2009 *The Times* published its list of 'most historically inaccurate movies'; *Braveheart* came second.

Braveheart had a massive effect on tourism in Scotland, while its nationalist, anti-English outlook has influenced popular Scottish politics for almost two decades.

The flipside to what might be termed 'movies about men in kilts' is a series of films with a defiantly urban, contemporary edge – after all, the majority of Scots live in cities, not in picturesque lochside hamlets. Prime examples include Danny Boyle's first two films – the dark noir of *Shallow Grave* (1995) and the squalor and heroin-humour of *Trainspotting* (1996).

FILM LOCATIONS

You could happily spend many months pottering around Scotland looking for locations used in movies; the dramatic landscapes, varied topography and preserved historical settings have proved to be a magnet for filmmakers of all genres.

Probably the most-filmed location is Eilean Donan Castle (Lochalsh, Highland). Thanks to the movies, the reconstructed castle's island setting in a sea loch is now an icon of Scotland. The medieval castle was blown up by Government troops in 1719 as a reprisal for Jacobite activities (Spanish soldiers had been garrisoned there during the entirely abortive rising of that year, culminating in the Jacobite defeat at the Battle of Glenshiel). What visitors see today is a faux-medieval Edwardian baronial-style Romantic recreation built between 1912 and 1932.

The Thirty-Nine Steps, an exciting espionage adventure novel written in 1915 by the redoubtable Scottish author John Buchan, has been filmed no less than four times. The 1935 version, directed by Alfred Hitchcock and featuring an iconic escape on the Forth Rail Bridge, is widely regarded as one of the greatest British movies of all time. The 1959 version is the one to choose for Scottish locations, however, as numerous scenes were filmed in and around Edinburgh, and in Perth & Kinross and the Trossachs area of Stirling District, most notably the Falls of Dochart at Killin. The 1978 film is the one closest to the plot of Buchan's original novel, and shows a number of locations in Dumfries & Galloway, while the 2008 film was shot entirely on location in Scotland, and features Stirling Castle, Bo'ness (Falkirk District), Glasgow, and a German U-boat in Loch Katrine (Stirling District).

James Bond has been active in Scotland ever since his fictional biography shows him being expelled as a boy from Fettes College in Edinburgh. The helicopter and boat chase scenes in *From Russia With Love* (1963) were filmed around Crinan and Lochgilhead in Argyll. In the rather bizarre spoof *Casino Royale* (1967), David Niven as 'the real James Bond' survives a SMERSH sex attack at a Scottish castle. *The Spy Who Loved Me* (1977) includes the Gare Loch submarine base on the Clyde. For *The World is Not Enough* (1999) Eilean Donan Castle is MI6's temporary HQ, 'Castle Thane', where Q shows Bond a set of bagpipes that is actually a machine gun. And, most evocatively of all, in *Skyfall* (2012) Bond is depicted as having a Scottish estate as his family home. The fight scenes in the house were actually done in Surrey, although some spectacular landscape scenes were filmed in Glen Coe and Glen Etive in the Western Highlands.

Gregory's Girl (1981), possibly the best coming-of-age story in British cinema, was filmed in and around a secondary school in the new town of Cumbernauld (North Lanarkshire). For the American release, the Scottish accents of the original cast were overdubbed with more 'user-friendly' Anglicised versions.

Gregory's Girl director, Bill Forsyth, also made the wonderful comedy *Local Hero* (1983), which was principally filmed at Pennan (Aberdeenshire) and Camusdarach beach (Morar, Highland). Felix Happer, the film's eccentric American oil executive played by Burt Lancaster, has an asteroid named after him: 7345 Happer.

The otter-tastic *Ring of Bright Water* (1969) was filmed on the Isle of Seil, near Oban (Argyll), which bears a resemblance to the landscape of Sandaig on the west coast opposite Skye, the setting for author Gavin Maxwell's original autobiographical book.

Edinburgh's best-loved dog has not been best served by cinema. The studio-set *Greyfriars Bobby* (1961) is so sickly sweet it could rot your teeth. *The Adventures of Greyfriars Bobby* (2005) thinks that Stirling Castle is the same place as Edinburgh Castle, and that the lowland county of East Lothian is somehow next door to the Scottish Highlands at the other end of the country. In addition, although Bobby was a Skye terrier, the film uses a West Highland terrier – because the latter was 'cuter'.

Things on film are not always what they seem. The 'Appalachian Mountains' shown in the 2005 horror movie *The Descent* are not in America but were filmed in the Central Highlands around Dunkeld in Perth & Kinross. The extraordinary epic *Cloud Atlas* (2012) uses Glasgow and other locations as a substitute for San Francisco, while 'Philadelphia' in the zombie apocalypse movie *World War Z* (2013) is, again, actually Glasgow. The helicopter attack on the train heading into the Channel Tunnel in *Mission Impossible* (1996) was filmed, not in Kent, but on the railway line between Kilmarnock and Dumfries.

The supposedly Highland setting for the werewolf horror film *Dog Soldiers* (2002) was actually filmed in Norway and Luxembourg.

The original intention of filming *Brigadoon* (1954) on location was abandoned when Gene Kelly, the film's star, travelled to Scotland and realised just how bad the weather could be. The MGM studio was substituted instead, which is why this musical, about a Highland village that only reappears for one day every century, has enough visual Scottish clichés to build a wee thatched cottage out of shortbread and haggis.

Scotland, of course, is replete with castles, stately homes and historic buildings; a veritable gift for filmmakers. Rosslyn Chapel (East Lothian) featured in *The Da Vinci Code* (2006). Dunnotar Castle (Aberdeenshire) and Blackness Castle (West Lothian) atmospherically stood in for Elsinore in *Hamlet* (1990), while Blackness was also central to *Macbeth* (1997) and *Doomsday* (2008). *Greystoke: the Legend of Tarzan, King of the Apes* (1984) features Floors Castle (Scottish Borders) as the Greystoke family seat, and *The Queen* (2006) makes use not only of Blairquhan and Culzean Castles in South Ayrshire and Castle Fraser (Aberdeenshire), but also – given that this is about the Royal Family – Queen Elizabeth II's Scottish home at Balmoral.

2001 saw the first Bollywood movie set and filmed in Scotland, a love story about an Indian student studying in the country, with locations including Stirling Castle and the University of Glasgow, as well as Loch Lomond and Culzean Castle (South Ayrshire). The opening musical number of an earlier Bollywood hit, *Kuch Kuch Hota Hai* (1998), features short clips of Eilean Donan Castle and the island-based Inchmahome Priory (Stirling District).

Whisky Galore! (1949), in which a shipwrecked whisky cargo brings joy to a Scottish island, remains one of the best-loved Ealing comedies. Filmed on Barra in the Western Isles, the movie, like the novel from which it was adapted, was based on the real-life wreck of the SS *Politician* off the island of Eriskay in 1941. Whisky that was not purloined by the wily locals was in reality blown up with dynamite by customs officials. The wreck of the *Politician* still lies off Eriskay.

The fantasy film *Highlander* (1986) tells the story of an immortal clansman from the sixteenth century, and features Highland locations around Skye, Glen Coe, Torridon and (yet again!) Eilean Donan Castle. The sweep and dramatic power of the Scottish landscape has proved to be a draw for many purveyors of fantasy and science fiction, from *Dragonslayer* and *Quest for Fire* (both 1981) to *Stardust* (2007) and *The Dark Knight Rises* (2012). The extraordinary, otherworldly area around the Old Man of Storr on Skye is a particular favourite, and often features in aerial scenes such as those in *The Land that Time Forgot* (1975), *Snow White and the Huntsman* and *Prometheus* (both 2012).

The *Harry Potter* films have made gleeful use of Scottish scenery to achieve the right sense of mystery and majesty. Glen Coe and Glen Nevis feature extensively, while the Hogwarts Express steams across the iconic twenty-one arches of the Glenfinnan Viaduct (Lochaber/Highland), which has made the latter a must-see destination for fans.

What many regard as the best British horror film ever made has left an unusual legacy in Scotland. At Burrow Head in Dumfries & Galloway are the feet of one of the huge wooden figures burned at the human-sacrificial climax of *The Wicker Man* (1973). The remains, along with other Wicker Man locations in the south-west and at Plockton near Skye, have become places of pilgrimage for devoted fans of the cult movie that featured Edward Woodward and Christopher Lee.

Scotland continues to act as a suitable backdrop for adventure and marvels. The 2012 animated fantasy *Brave*, for example, which could have conceivably have been set anywhere in medieval Europe, was placed very firmly in the Scottish Highlands.

THEATRE

Peter Pan, the 'boy who wouldn't grow up', originally appeared in a novel, *The Little White Bird*, in 1902, before debuting on stage in 1904, going on to became a huge, world-spanning hit. Neverland, the Lost Boys, Wendy, Captain Hook – all were the creation of a very short, very shy weaver's son from Kirriemuir in Angus. J.M. Barrie's childhood play-acting in the gardens of Moat Brae house in Dumfries was the inspiration for Peter Pan's pirates, and Moat Brae is currently being developed, appropriately, as a centre for children's literature.

Edmund Kean, one of the stars of the Georgian theatre world, built Woodend House on the Isle of Bute so he could escape from both hostile audiences and his creditors. On the other side of the island lies the grave of Montague Stanley, an actor who gave up the theatre because he thought it was too sinful; he died in 1844 and is the only occupant of the churchyard at Ascog.

8

THE NATURAL WORLD

THE ROCKS REMAIN

Geology as a modern science was born in Scotland. In the late eighteenth century, James Hutton realised for the first time that a set of rock layers lying close together at different angles meant that the rocks were actually from different periods in Earth's distant history. Hutton identified such unconformities at Barns Ness in East Lothian and on the Isle of Arran, and published his ideas in his 1787 book *Theory of the Earth*, where he made the revolutionary claim that mountains were uplifted and then eroded over millions of years – a slight contrast to the story of the six days of creation from the Bible.

Arran remains popular with geological field trips, as the island provides spectacular examples of the effect of the Ice Ages, from U-shaped valleys and raised beaches to glacial erratics – huge granite boulders that were transported from the mountains to the coast by the power of the glaciers.

Rockhounds also like to take their holidays on Skye, Mull and in Torridon in the north-west, all of which are geological marvels.

From space, the most obvious feature of Scotland is the Great Glen, a trench that marks a major fault system from Inverness to Fort William, and virtually bisects the Highlands along a north-east – south-west line. The 60-mile-long valley is home to four lochs (including Loch Ness) and the Caledonian Canal.

An area of rocks near Assynt in the north-west Highlands, known as the Lewisian Gneiss Complex, dates from one of the key moments in the history of the planet – the formation of the continental crust, nearly 3 billion years ago.

EARTHQUAKES

Scotland can hardly be compared with earthquake centres such as Japan and California. Nevertheless, the ground does shake on occasion. There may have been a major quake on 18 September 1508, although the records are sparse and it seems that the epicentre was in the sea off the Western Isles, so damage was light.

Shocks were felt all over the Highlands in 1597, Comrie in western Perthshire was hit by dozens of quakes in the eighteenth and nineteenth centuries, and several people died when houses collapsed in Inverness in 1769.

The centre of quake activity is the west and north-west Highlands, where five quakes occurred between 2011 and 2013.

The Orkney Islands are virtually earthquake-free zones.

The world's first seismometer was invented in Perthshire in 1841. The tiny Earthquake House in Comrie now recalls the pioneering early days of recording earth tremors.

The British Geological Survey maintains two seismological measuring stations in Scotland, one at Lerwick in Shetland and the other at Eskdalemuir in the Scottish Borders. Both also record meteorological observations, solar radiation and atmospheric pollution, among a number of other physical geodata. The Eskdalemuir Observatory was built in 1908 to replace a station at Kew in London, where electric tramcars were interfering with the measurements.

The well-known personality David Icke predicted that the Isle of Arran would be hit by a devastating earthquake before the end of 1991, and would sink beneath the waves. This event has yet to take place.

DINOSAURS

The first evidence of a Scottish dinosaur was uncovered in 1982, when a footprint of a Jurassic herbivore was found on Skye. Ten years later saw the first discovery of a dinosaur bone in Scotland, again on Skye.

The Staffin Museum on Skye now has the largest collection of Scottish dinosaur fossils in the country.

A full-size Tyrannosaurus Rex stands near Brodick on Arran. The slightly bizarre model dates from the 1970s.

Another T-Rex once glared balefully from outside the Hunterian Museum in Glasgow. Installed in 2001 as part of a dinosaur exhibition, it proved so popular that it remained in place for four years after the exhibition closed.

Several locations around Loch Ness sport large fibreglass creatures clearly modelled on the plesiosaur, the long-necked prehistoric marine

reptile that has become popularly associated with the Loch Ness Monster. Loch Ness is far too cold for any reptile, never mind a huge beast that's been extinct for 60 million years, but there you go.

WILD, WILD LIFE

In 2010, wildlife tourism – including bird watching, whale watching and guided walks – was estimated to be worth £127 million a year to the Scottish economy. Dolphin watching in the north-east brings in £4 million to local purses each year, while some £2 million is spent on Mull by people hoping to catch a glimpse of the island's renowned sea eagles.

Scotland is home to 400,000 examples of the largest native land animal in Britain – the red deer. The sight of a group of stags on the hillside is something never to be forgotten. Also unforgettable – especially if you are trying to sleep – is the incredibly loud 'rut roar' made by the stags during the mating season.

Red deer became iconically linked with Scotland through the popularity of Sir Edwin Landseer's Victorian painting *Monarch of the Glen*. The image of the majestically-antlered stag was used in the advertising for Dewar's and Glenfiddich whisky, and hence the equation 'whisky = stag = Scotland' was established around the world. The painting can be admired to this day in the National Museum of Scotland in Edinburgh.

The much smaller roe deer – also a native species – can be distinguished by the white patch on their rumps as they bound away from you.

Bottlenose dolphins can regularly be seen disporting in the Moray Firth (the most northerly point in the world for these mammals), while common dolphins and harbour porpoises are also frequent visitors. Orcas (killer whales) and minke whales are often sighted around Shetland and the north-west coast.

You could spend a lifetime in Scotland and never see some of its more elusive native mammals, such as the badger, pine marten or Scottish wildcat. The wildcat's existence as a pure species is under threat because wildcats regularly interbreed with feral domestic cats.

In the 1960s the world's most famous otters lived at Sandaig in Lochalsh, where author Gavin Maxwell immortalized Mij, Edal and Teko in his bestselling books *Ring of Bright Water*, *The Rocks Remain* and *Raven Seek Thy Brother*.

Just south of Helmsdale on the A9 a memorial stone reads: 'To mark the place near which (according to Scrope's 'Art of Deerstalking') the last wolf in Sutherland was killed by the hunter Polson in or about the year 1700.' This is just one of at least a dozen 'last wolf' stories to be found across Scotland – as wolves became scarcer, the number of such stories increased. 'Last wolves' were allegedly killed at Killiecrankie (Perth & Kinross, 1690), Loch Ruthven near Loch Ness (about 1700), Strathglass in Highland Region (about 1700), the Black Wood of Rannoch in Perth & Kinross (early eighteenth century) and near the River Findhorn in Moray (1743).

There is a credible report that a single wolf was seen in the Dionard valley of Sutherland as late as 1888.

The MacDonalds of Glen Clunie in Aberdeenshire were supposedly descended from a man who had been raised by wolves. In nearby Glen Muic a variant of the story was told – there the MacDonald ancestor was brought up by wild boar.

In 1893 the folklorist Walter Traill Dennison published an article about an unnamed family on Orkney who claimed to be descended from a liaison between a human woman and a selkie – a shapeshifting were-seal that can temporarily shed its sealskin to come on land. For generations mothers in the family clipped off the seal-like webs that spread between the fingers and toes of their children. According to the article, the webs, unable to grow naturally, developed into a horny crust – and Dennison himself saw living examples of men and women from the family with these disfiguring horny growths on their hands and feet.

There may be some 100,000 grey seals around the coast of Scotland, and perhaps a quarter of that number of common seals. Take a boat trip and you may well see seals hauled out on rocks or beaches, taking a snooze before heading off in search of a fish supper.

A grey seal can live for up to forty-five years.

If you're in western coastal waters and spot something large cruising around with a shark-like dorsal fin and a huge open mouth, you're lucky enough to have seen a basking shark, an entirely harmless (and toothless) giant fish that filters plankton through its gaping maw.

Since the nineteenth century, locals have been gulling tourists with tales that haggis (the food) is actually the body of a rarely glimpsed creature, the wild Highland Haggis. In 2005 the staff of the Kelvingrove Art Gallery and Museum in Glasgow created a composite creature from the various parts of several different animals, and put it on display as a rare specimen of the legendary *Haggis scoticus.*

BIRD-BRAINED

The Scottish crossbill, which likes hanging from trees upside down, is the only bird that is found in Scotland and nowhere else in the world.

The Bass Rock in the Firth of Forth is the world's largest rock gannetry, hosting 40,000 pairs of Northern Gannets. If you pass the island on a boat trip, the smell will reach you before the noise does.

Parts of Orkney are well known for the skuas that will dive-bomb walkers who get too close.

There are 230 breeding pairs of golden eagles in Scotland.

Generations of dippers have been laying eggs in the same nest site near Dumfries since 1881.

The last Great Auk in Britain was killed off St Kilda in 1840 – by three local men who believed it was a witch that had raised a storm. The species became entirely extinct around the world twelve years later.

PLEASE ALLOW ME TO INTRODUCE MYSELF

Many plants and animals have been introduced into Scotland by humans, for better or worse.

There are 988 alien species in Scotland. 84 per cent are plants, while forty-nine species of birds and thirteen species of mammals are on the list, along with sixteen fish, twenty-two insects, fifty molluscs and one amphibian.

Some aliens, such as the brown hare – deliberately introduced by the Romans as a food source in the fourth century – and the Orkney vole, which hitchhiked with Neolithic settlers from Europe around 3500 BC, have been here for so long they are part of the scenery, or 'naturalised'. Most others have little impact on the environment. A small number of introduced animals and plants, however, become invasive, out-competing or destroying native species and threatening not just biodiversity but economic well-being.

The North American signal crayfish, originally a restaurant breed, was first recorded in the wild in Galloway in 1995, and has now colonised large areas of fresh water in the south-west. The signal crayfish is ecologically aggressive and preys on other species, and poses a threat to economically important fish such as Atlantic salmon and brown trout.

American Mink were introduced as a lucrative fur-farming animal, in cages that were supposedly escape-proof. Today hundreds of mink live in the wild in Scotland, annihilating native populations of fish, water voles and ground-nesting birds. A massive project is currently underway to attempt to eliminate mink from north and north-east Scotland.

In the five years up to 2007, £500,000 was spent on the River Tweed to control invasive non-native plants such as Japanese knotweed and giant hogweed. The cost of clearing the invasive *Rhododendron ponticum* from the Loch Lomond and Trossachs National Park is estimated at £25 million.

The hedgehog is native to Scotland, but not to the Western Isles. When it was introduced there in the late twentieth century – apparently because it was 'cute' – the hedgehogs' penchant for bird eggs saw the population of wading birds such as dunlin crash by 75 per cent.

The introduction of North American grey squirrels in 1892 has been a disaster for the native red squirrels, which have declined severely in recent years.

There is a colony of red-necked wallabies in Loch Lomond. The Australian marsupials were introduced there in the 1970s, and seem to cause few problems, probably because they are confined to a small island.

The only amphibian alien in Scotland is the alpine newt. This was released in 1957 when a research facility at the University of Edinburgh simply found it had too many.

Even some of what might be regarded as classic 'sights' of Scotland are not native. Two of the four species of deer in Scotland – sika and fallow – were introduced simply as hunting fodder, as were pheasants (introduced from Asia) and partridges (introduced from Europe). The anglers' favourite, rainbow trout, is not native, and was first released for sport in 1888.

... AND WE'RE BACK!

The red kite, the white-tailed sea eagle, the northern goshawk and the capercaillie all became extinct in Scotland in recent times as a result of human activities. All have been successfully reintroduced.

Reindeer were native to northern Scotland until the early Middle Ages. A Swedish reindeer herder reintroduced reindeer into the Cairngorms in 1952, with a second group brought in to the Cromdale Hills in 1990. Strictly managed so that their population does not damage the ecosystem, the free-ranging animals can be visited at feeding times, weather (and reindeer behaviour) permitting.

At Christmas, some of the Cairngorm reindeer are used to pull Santa's sleigh. None of the animals has yet developed a red nose.

Beavers were hunted to extinction in Scotland in the sixteenth century. In 2009 they made a triumphant return, being reintroduced in the Knapdale area of Argyll.

Ospreys became extinct in Britain in 1916. In 1954 a pair of Scandinavian birds started breeding in Scotland of their own accord, and there are now at least four locations in the country where ospreys breed regularly. In a grim comment on the idiocy of a few humans, the exact location of some nests is not publicised, to prevent the eggs being stolen by people who call themselves egg collectors, but are nothing less than criminals.

The various successful reintroduction programmes have buoyed the hopes of some people who want to see the return of lynx. The big cats were indigenous to Scotland until the Dark Ages, when humans

wiped them out. However, not many landowners would welcome the return of a large feline predator.

There are rumblings – but no official plans – to reintroduce the brown bear (extinction date in Scotland: tenth century), the elk (extinction date: fourteenth century), and the wolf (extinction date: eighteenth century, probably). Wild boar (extinct from the sixteenth century) have recently been reintroduced to a single enclosed area in the Highlands.

No one has yet suggested the reintroduction of polar bears, woolly rhinoceroses or woolly mammoths, all of which once roamed Scotland during the Ice Ages.

THE FLY IN THE OINTMENT

Whether living in or visiting Scotland, it is possible you may not encounter any of the indigenous or introduced species mentioned above. There is one creature, however, that you will find hard to avoid, especially in the Highlands in summer – the dreaded midge.

The Highland Midge – known more accurately as the Scottish Biting Midge – is a tiny bloodsucking fly that frequently appears in vast swarms. It can make some outdoor activities impossible. In 1872 Queen Victoria sat down for a Highland picnic – and was 'eaten alive' by midges.

Researchers have found that midges prefer tall men (because the insects fly above head height and land on the tallest first) and overweight people (probably because they produce more midge-attracting carbon dioxide and lactic acid). A lucky 15 per cent of people seem to have a natural midge-repellent as part of their body chemistry.

Should you be able to stand in a midge cloud for an hour, wearing minimal clothing and eschewing insect repellent, you would receive perhaps 40,000 bites.

DOMESTICATED ANIMALS

The Soay sheep is a primitive breed related to the early domesticated sheep of the Neolithic and Bronze Age. A large and entirely unmanaged herd of these hardy beasts lives on the island of Hirta in the St Kilda archipelago. With no other sheep leaving or arriving on the island, and with an absence of predators, the Soay population is a perfect subject for scientific study. Typically, the sheep breed until the environment can no longer sustain their numbers – and then the population crashes. In 1989, over just twelve weeks, their numbers fell by two-thirds – at which point the boom-and-bust cycle started all over again.

The largest single-day sheep sale in Europe can be found in the remote Highland community of Lairg in Sutherland, where hundreds of farmers and thousands of sheep congregate every August.

The Aberdeen Angus breed was developed from the black cattle of north-east Scotland by three far-sighted cattle farmers in the nineteenth century, and today is probably the best-known quality beef brand in the world.

The late Queen Mother was the patron of the Aberdeen Angus Cattle Society, and her herd still thrives at the Castle of Mey in Caithness (Highland). The current patron, Prince Charles, has his own Aberdeen Angus herd at his farm in Highgrove, Gloucestershire.

The Shetland pony is one of the smallest pony breeds in the world, with some adults being less than 2½ft tall. No one knows how old the breed actually is, although it retains some characteristics from prehistoric ponies. Hardy and strong – able to pull twice their own weight – Shetland ponies can sometimes live for up to thirty years. In the nineteenth century, many Shetland ponies led short, grim lives as pit ponies in British and American coalmines – thankfully these days are long past.

If you want to see mountain goats, head for the remote fastness of Diabaig in Wester Ross (Highland). During a cattle shortage the villagers took to keeping goats. These have now turned feral, and can often be seen adding another picturesque element to the fantastic Torridon scenery.

Many modern breeds of dog have their origins in Scotland. Most derive from the needs of country dwellers in previous times, principally livestock herding, vermin control and hunting. The tall,

loping Scottish Deerhound was bred, not surprisingly, to chase deer. Other dogs originally bred for hunting and/or ratting include the Cairn Terrier, the Skye Terrier, the Border Terrier and the Golden Retriever.

The Dandie Dimont Terrier is named after a character in Sir Walter Scott's 1815 novel *Guy Mannering*.

Herding dogs from Scotland include the Sheltie (Shetland Sheepdog), the Bearded Collie, the Smooth Collie, and the Rough Collie. If you can't bring the appearance of a Rough Collie to mind, here's a clue – Lassie.

In his 1994 book *The Intelligence of Dogs*, psychology professor Stanley Coren concluded that Border Collies were amongst the world's smartest dogs. The popular black-and-white breed originated as a working dog on the farms of the Scottish Borders, and has attained Olympic levels in dog sports and sheepdog trials.

Perhaps the iconic Scottish breed is the West Highland White Terrier. 'Westies' are hugely popular pets, and are visually associated with the advertising for Cesar dog food and the Black & White brand of whisky, as well as with one of BBC Scotland's 'greatest hits', the much-loved TV drama series *Hamish Macbeth*.

As with most dog breeds, the origins of the West Highland Terrier are a little confused, but Westies probably date from the first few years of the twentieth century.

The only Scottish cat breed is the Scottish Fold, which has ears that bend down and forward, giving it an owlish look. The fold is an accidental mutation, and the breed originates from a single cat found in Coupar Angus, Perth & Kinross, in 1961.

SIGNIFICANT TREES

Scotland's rarest native trees are the Arran whitebeam and the Arran cut-leaved whitebeam, both of which only grow in one place in the world – the Isle of Arran. Both species are perilously close to extinction.

McCulloch's Tree on the Isle of Mull is a fossil imprint some 40ft high and 50 million years old. Getting to it requires a full day's strenuous walk.

When the final Ice Age ended, Scotland was quickly forested – some 70 per cent of the country becoming carpeted by Scots pines by 6000 BC. The pine forests retreated around 2000 BC when the climate became cooler and wetter, and the ancient Caledonian Forest has since been further eroded by human activities.

No one knows where the oldest living Scots pine might be, but the oldest that has been scientifically dated was a seedling planted in the 1440s, when James II was on the throne. Several other trees around its remote location in Glen Loyne (Highland) are at least 440 years old.

The oldest Scots pines that can be easily visited are in Ballochbuie Forest, part of the Balmoral Estate in Aberdeenshire. The 400-year-old trees owe their survival to Queen Victoria, who bought the forest to prevent the trees being felled for timber. The Ballochbuie pinewood is one of the largest remnants of the primordial Caledonian Forest remaining today.

The oldest living thing not just in Scotland, but in Europe, is the Fortingall Yew in Perth & Kinross. It is estimated to be 5,000 years old. The once-vast central trunk has largely vanished (blame eighteenth- and nineteenth-century vandalism), but the several peripheral secondary trunks are all in good health.

The Gordon Castle Ash in Moray was planted perhaps in the late 1700s, making it much, much older than the average ash (which rarely survive past their 200th birthday). The oldest tulip tree in the country may be the one planted in what is now Hirsel Country Park (Scottish Borders) in 1740. And dating from 1550, the Newbattle Abbey Sycamore in Midlothian was the oldest specimen in the UK – until a freak gust of wind blew it down in 2006.

Old trees attract legends like an old house attracts ghost stories. Despite being several hundred years old, the Birnam Oak in Perth & Kinross, aka Macbeth's Oak, is still far too young to have been part of the Birnam Wood that, according to Shakespeare (and no one else), supposedly provided camouflage for Malcolm's attack on Macbeth's stronghold at Dunsinane in the eleventh century. Likewise, the Wallace Yew in Elderslie, Renfrewshire, may possibly be growing near where William Wallace was born, but it was not around in Wallace's day, as it is a mere 400 years old.

A tree in south-west Glasgow bears a sign reading, 'Henry Stewart, Lord Darnley and Mary, Queen of Scots, sat under this great sycamore tree when she nursed him back to health after an illness.' Like a great many claims associated with Mary, this is a fib: the tree is only a couple of hundred years old, so it couldn't have been providing shelter in 1565 when Mary and her second husband supposedly stayed at nearby Crookston Castle.

On the other hand, it is just possible that Rizzio's Chestnut at Melville Castle in Midlothian was indeed planted in the 1560s by Mary's private secretary David Rizzio. Rizzio was later murdered in front of the queen at Holyrood Palace; however, the 450-year-old sweet chestnut is still doing well.

Although the King James II Holly at Floors Castle in the Scottish Borders at first appears to be too young to have been around when James died here in 1460, closer inspection shows a decayed stump which may indeed date back to the Middle Ages. During a siege, a cannon exploded and fatally wounded the king, and the holly is said to mark the spot where he expired.

The Brahan Elm in Easter Ross (Highland), dating from 1735, is Britain's largest wych elm, with a girth of 23ft. As the owner of the same-sized waistline, the most girthsome Douglas fir in the country is at Dunkeld in Perth & Kinross. The Ardkinglas Silver fir at Loch Fyne in Argyll has a girth of 32ft and, with a volume of almost 5,000 cubic feet of wood, is one of the bulkiest trees in Europe.

A line of sixteen giant sequoia trees at the House of Dun in Angus so dominate the flat landscape that sailors use them as a navigational aid.

The tallest tree in Scotland? Take your pick from: the Hermitage Douglas fir in Perth & Kinross (over 201ft); Dughall Mor ('the big dark stranger'), a Douglas Fir at Reelig Glen, west of Inverness (about 204ft); the Grand Fir at Blair Atholl, Perth & Kinross (between 205 and 206ft); and the current champion, the Stronardon Douglas fir in Argyll (about 209ft). The title holder of tallest tree shifts over the years, as trees do insist on growing.

'Dool' trees were natural gallows, ideal for supporting a rope during impromptu public hangings. Dool means grief or sorrow. Some dool trees still remain, notably at Blairquhan Castle and Kilkerran House (both South Ayrshire), Cessnock Castle (East Ayrshire), Leith Hall and Haugh of Glass (both Aberdeenshire), Loch Rannoch and Logierait (both Perth & Kinross) and Drumnadrochit (Loch Ness).

Palm trees. Sub-tropical tree ferns. Exotic plants from the Southern Hemisphere. Yes, you're still in Scotland – at the Logan Botanic Garden in Galloway, to be precise, where the balmy influence of the Gulf Stream allows warmth-loving species to flourish outdoors.

The Twin Trees, a pair of Scots pines at Finzean in Aberdeenshire, have grown into each other, forming a natural wooden arch.

Driving along the A82 between Glencoe and Bridge of Orchy, you'll pass the loneliest tree in Scotland. A single rowan has managed to establish itself on a boulder in the otherwise treeless landscape of Rannoch Moor, and as such has become a well-known landmark on this desolate stretch.

A sycamore at Brig o'Turk (Stirling District) eats iron. Over the past hundred years it has swallowed up an anchor and a bicycle – of the latter, only the handlebars are still visible. The Wishing Tree in wildest Argyll was a spectacularly shaped, wind-blasted hawthorn, now dead, where travellers pushed coins into the trunk while making a wish. A beech in Luncarty, Perth & Kinross, functioned as a toothache tree, where nails hammered into the trunk 'transferred' the pain of the toothache to the tree.

THISTLE AND I'LL COME TO YOU

The Scottish national floral emblem is the thistle. No one really knows why.

According to tradition – and who can argue with that? – a party of Vikings were creeping up on a Scots army at night when one of the barefooted attackers stepped on the prickly weed and cried out, thus giving the game away and allowing the Scots to bash a goodly number of Viking heads. Several locations the length and breadth of Scotland lay claim to be the very spot where this crucial event took place, although there is not the slightest scrap of evidence to support the story, never mind the individual candidates.

There are six thistle species that are contenders for the 'Scottish thistle': the cotton thistle, the melancholy thistle, the musk thistle, Our Lady's thistle, the spear thistle and the stemless thistle. Which one is the official national symbol? No one knows, or at least no one can agree on the same one.

HEATHERS

The tough climate and infertile soils of the Highlands form the perfect environment for the growth of the flowering low shrub known as heather. Heather covers much of upland and moorland Scotland, creating a purple carpet during the twice-yearly bloom.

Not surprisingly, heather has come to be used as a symbol or shorthand for Highland Scotland. To choose but one example, Eric Linklater's 1965 book (and its accompanying television documentary) about Bonnie Prince Charlie's escape through the Highlands and Islands was simply called *The Prince in the Heather*.

White heather, as distinct from purple heather, is relatively rare, and hence developed a sense that it was somehow 'lucky'. Queen Victoria recorded a Highlander leaping from a carriage to pluck a spring of white heather he had spied while passing by. White heather correspondingly became a standard element in a bridal bouquet.

For eleven years from 1957, BBC Television broadcast *The White Heather Club*, an early-evening variety show. By chance, it was one of the first BBC programmes to be recorded on videotape, and hence a few episodes can still be viewed today. Watching it, you will either be enveloped in nostalgic delight for a bevy of kilted Scottish light entertainers of days yore – Jimmy Shand, Andy Stewart, the Corries, and four dancers in tartan sashes, all named Heather – or, you will be aghast at the programme's 'Hoots, Mon!' tartanised and clichéd depiction of Scotland, a cod-Highland confection created in a studio in Glasgow.

THE WEATHER

In 1962 wind speeds of 177mph were registered on Unst in Shetland. This record speed might well have been higher – but the recording equipment was blown away.

On average, it rains for 250 days a year in the Highlands.

The maximum temperature ever recorded in Scotland is 32.9°C, an extraordinary event which took place in Greycook in the Scottish Borders during August 2003. Don't expect to come across temperatures anything like this – although 2013 saw the country swelter in a brief heatwave – as the summer average rarely reaches 22°C.

The coldest recorded temperature in the UK is -27.2°C, which hit Braemar (Aberdeenshire) in 1982 and Altnaharra (Sutherland/Highland) in 1995.

Scotland's high latitude means that daylight hours in summer are extraordinarily long – in Shetland you can sometimes read a newspaper outside at midnight. Of course, in winter, the reverse is

true – the nights in northern latitudes can last for up to eighteen hours. In compensation, winter is also the best time to see the Northern Lights – once again, Shetland is the place to be for the amazing auroral displays.

Scotland's maritime-island climate is characterised by extreme variability and unpredictability. There is a well-known saying: 'If you don't like the weather, just wait for five minutes.'

9

SCOTLAND AT WORK

Scotland has so many industries and other areas of economic activity that here only a handful can be skimmed. Until the mid-eighteenth century the vast majority of Scots worked in agriculture or fishing. A century later more people lived in the city of Glasgow than the whole of the Highlands and Islands. Large areas of the Lowlands suffered in the post-industrial decline of the post-war era, but the economy remains strong in sectors such as financial services, biotechnology and healthcare, offshore oil and gas production, and tourism.

SOME STATISTICS
ABOUT SCOTLAND'S ECONOMY
(WHICH ARE ACTUALLY QUITE INTERESTING)

Scotland's Gross Domestic Product, which is a way of estimating the annual value of the economy, is between £124 and £150 billion – the variation being caused by the different ways that economic statistics are gathered.

As of 2013, just over 2.5 million people in Scotland were in work, or around 72 per cent of the adult population.

758,000 people were 'economically inactive'. This included people who were unemployed, retired, sick or disabled, caring for others, or in full-time study.

Around 20 per cent of all households were 'workless' – that is, none of the adults in the household had any kind of employment.

Over 340,000 private sector businesses operate in Scotland. These vary from one-person sole traders to giants such as ScottishPower. More than 98 per cent of all private businesses had forty-nine or fewer employees, while another 1.1 per cent were medium enterprises with between 50 and 249 employees. Between them these two groups are known as Small and Medium-sized Enterprises (SMEs).

More than half of private sector employees work in SMEs.

Over 16 per cent of all Scottish businesses are in Construction, making this sector the largest in the private sector. The second largest private business sector is 'Professional, Scientific and Technical'.

Manufacturing, which in the early twentieth century was Scotland's largest business sector by far, is now well down the list, being eleventh in the statistics, below areas such as Retail, Transportation, and Accommodation and Food Services.

The largest single employer in Scotland, across both private and public sectors, is the National Health Service, which has around 150,000 employees.

TRADE

In the fifteenth century, Bruges in present-day Belgium was the 'staple' port for Scotland. This meant that Scottish merchants gained a number of profitable privileges in exchange for agreeing to sell their goods exclusively in the Flemish port. The principal Scottish export – and the reason why the burghers of Bruges were so keen to do business – was wool. In Flanders the raw wool was woven into high-quality cloth and tapestries, both of which fetched good prices across Europe. The words 'Flemish cloth' and 'Melrose wool' were the medieval equivalents of modern-day brand names like Armani or Burberry.

Scottish merchants established trading communities across Europe, from France to Russia. One of the more extraordinary export drives took place in the seventeenth century, when somewhere between 15,000 and 40,000 Scots were earning a living in Poland, largely as merchants, craftsmen and packmen (itinerant peddlers). Although long forgotten in Scotland, these economic migrants left a linguistic trace in Poland, with several present-day villages having Polish placename versions of 'Scotland' or 'Scottish' such as Szotniki, Szoty and Skotna Góra. You will also find Poles with surnames such as Ramzy (from the Scottish name Ramsay) or Czarmas (Chalmers).

Britain's oldest still-running business is the Aberdeen Harbour Board, which was established in 1136.

Aberdeen also lays claim to what may be the world's oldest transport company. The Shore Porters Society was founded in 1498, and is still going strong.

In terms of present-day exports sent by ship, Scotland's principal market is the Netherlands, which accounts for more than a quarter of all exports from Scottish ports. Germany, the USA and Belgium are the other main importers of goods shipped from Scotland.

Most ship-born imports currently arrive from Russia and Colombia, which each provide around 15 per cent of the total goods imported to Scotland by sea – with the majority being related to oil or fuel.

Most exports leave by the Forth ports; most imports arrive at the ports on the Clyde.

RICHES AND POVERTY

In 2013 a report by Oxfam stated that Scotland was one of the most unequal societies in the developed world. The wealthiest households were 273 times richer than the poorest.

In 2012, the 100 richest people in Scotland were worth £21 billion between them. This collective wealth had grown by £3 billion in the previous year.

The 'Glasgow Effect,' a recognised toxic mix of unemployment, poor diet, alcohol abuse, and low educational attainment, means that some men in poorer parts of the city have a life expectancy of only 62 years – fourteen years lower than the national male average. Women born in Scotland currently have a life expectancy of 80.1 years.

ENGINEERS

You could fill an entire book with the exploits of Scottish inventors and engineers.

James Watt, the pioneer of the steam engine, was born in Greenock and came to prominence in Glasgow. Without his world-changing ideas, the history of the Industrial Revolution would have been very different.

William Symington, who designed the world's first self-powered steamboat in 1789, was born at Leadhills in South Lanarkshire.

Thomas Telford, who built a good portion of industrial Britain and was the first president of the Institution of Civil Engineers, was born at Glendinning in Dumfries & Galloway. As well as the monument to him on the Eskdalemuir road, you can visit the churchyard of Bentpath and see the headstone the young Telford carved for his father's grave. Telford himself is buried in Westminster Abbey – a clear sign of the high regard in which he was held.

For a fascinating insight into a little-known aspect of Scotland's industrial heritage, visit the Denny Experimental Tank in Dumbarton. Here, scale models of the latest ships were tested in a 330ft long channel where stormy sea conditions were simulated.

John Logie Baird, the inventor of television, was born in Helensburgh (Argyll & Bute), and the town was also home to Henry Bell, designer of the *Comet*, the world's first seagoing steamship.

According to his official biography, *Star Trek*'s engineer Scotty ('the engines canna' take it, Captain!') will be born in Aberdeen in the year AD 2222. Chief Engineer Montgomery Scott will later distinguish himself under the leadership of Captain James T. Kirk on the starship *Enterprise*. The actor James Doohan based his character's accent on an Aberdonian he had met during the Second World War.

The fact that the Star Trek engineer is a Scot is an innate reflection of the worldwide reputation of Scottish engineering prowess.

IRON AND STEEL

The Carron Works, Falkirk, 1760: the first commercial iron-smelting furnace in Scotland starts up, only the second in Britain after Coalbrookdale in Shropshire. What had previously been the province of the village blacksmith or artisan armourer was now a mass-production operation. In many ways this was a crucial historical turning point, when the old world – the last Jacobite Rebellion had been crushed a mere fifteen years earlier – gave way to the new vision of the Industrial Revolution, a vast social change that saw Lowland Scotland become an industrialised heartland.

The Carron Works specialized in armaments, from cannons and mortars to chain-shot and carronades, the latter an anti-ship naval cannon named after their place of manufacture. HMS *Victory* used two 68-pounder carronades at the Battle of Trafalgar.

All the cannons and shot used by the Duke of Wellington at the Battle of Waterloo were manufactured at Carron.

If you lived in Victorian times and owned an iron stove, boiler, grate, drainpipe, pot or kettle, there was a good chance it had been cast at Carron.

By 1799 there were seventeen iron furnaces in Scotland. As these and other industries expanded, so did the towns and cities. Thousands of Highlanders migrated to the Lowlands in search of work, and iron-making on an industrial scale transformed society, from architecture and the tools used to erect buildings, to the creation of canals, railways and ships. Building ships with iron started on the Clyde in 1818, and grew to become one of the great enterprises of the industrial age.

MINING

Coal miners in seventeenth- and eighteenth-century Scotland were effectively slaves. They had to work in their 'home' mine for their entire life, they could not leave or change jobs, and their children were by law required to follow their parents in perpetual servitude. Boys who were not strong enough for the coalface were sold as servants. Generations of human beings were regarded as property, and bought and sold as part of the equipment and facilities when the colliery changed owners. Men employed at saltworks were similarly enslaved.

Scottish colliers were not legally freed from bondage until 1799.

Mining has always been an inherently dangerous occupation. Hundreds of men died in accidents throughout the nineteenth and twentieth centuries. In some cases courage and valour was recognised by official awards. The Edward Medal was instituted in 1907 as a means of recognising acts of bravery by miners, quarrymen and industrial workers; the first Scottish recipients were James and George Dryburgh, who in 1907 rescued two men overcome by poisonous gas in Lochhead Colliery near Coaltown of Wemyss in Fife.

In 1917 six miners spent nine hours trying to rescue a colleague from a collapsed shaft at Cowdenbeath Colliery in Fife; all were in constant danger for their lives. David Baird, John Boyle, George Shearer Christie, James Erskine, Edward McCafferty and Andrew Scott were all awarded the Edward Medal First Class.

In 1967 a fire broke out at the Michael Colliery in Fife, endangering the 316 men working underground. Nine died as a result of the thick black smoke. For their heroism in getting others to safety, David Hunter and Andrew Taylor were awarded the George Medal and the Edward Medal respectively. Andrew Taylor's award was posthumous, as he had gone back into the smoke to find some missing men, and was never seen alive again.

High up on the moors of East Ayrshire stand the few remains of Benwhat, an extraordinarily remote village once owned by the National Coal Board. At 1,100ft above sea level, this bleak mining outpost once had a school with eighty pupils, a championship-winning silver band, and a beer and whisky store where only men were allowed through the door. The village was abandoned in 1951.

OIL AND GAS

Bathgate, West Lothian, 1850: Dr James Young sets up the world's first commercial oilworks, refining paraffin, naphtha and oils from locally mined shale and coal; the global petroleum industry is born. 'Paraffin' Young was later the anonymous financial backer of David Livingstone's expeditions into Africa.

Undersea reserves of oil beneath the North Sea were first discovered in 1966, with full production commencing a decade later. Since then, the offshore oil and gas industry has transformed the economy and infrastructure of Scotland's east coast, particularly in Aberdeen, the 'oil capital'.

The oil and gas industry is economically the most important industrial sector in Scotland. It employs around 200,000 people, many of whom work for the 2,000 companies operating at every level of the supply chain in this global business.

Scottish oil and gas technology and expertise is exported to over 100 countries.

The North Sea is an unforgiving environment – cold, dark, deep, and subject to extreme weather. The challenges and technological solutions required by ultra-deep water work are equivalent to sending a mission into outer space.

On 6 July 1988 the oil rig Piper Alpha was ripped apart by explosions and fire. 167 men died. More than 100 changes were subsequently made to safety practices as a result of the lessons learned from the disaster. There is a moving memorial in Aberdeen's Hazlehead Garden.

THE 'LECCY

When the national electricity network in Scotland was built from the 1940s onwards, the planners not surprisingly concentrated on providing power to the areas of greatest use – the cities and industrial areas of the Lowlands. The recent rise in renewable energy schemes in the Highlands, however, has meant that the network in the north of Scotland does not have the capacity to handle the green energy now being produced. As a result, the upgrade of the network is the largest engineering project seen in Scotland for a generation.

There are only three organisations licensed to transmit electricity on high-voltage lines. The National Grid is responsible for the whole of England and Wales, while Scotland is split between ScottishPower (in the south) and Scottish Hydro Electric (in the north).

The tallest electricity pylons in Scotland are on the banks of the River Forth; their exceptional height of 430ft is required to allow the lines to cross the river safely.

A story dating from the construction of Highland hydroelectric schemes in the 1950s says that a workman, well over the alcohol limit, escaped from the police vehicle pursuing him by driving his car into the newlybuilt reservoir. If the story is true, the car may possibly still be there.

THE POST

The oldest working post office in the world can be found in Sanquhar, in Dumfries & Galloway. When it was established in 1712 letters

were delivered only by runner, and the postage cost was equivalent to a day's wages for a working man.

In 1934 an inventor in the Outer Hebrides experimented with delivering the mail by rocket. The short boat crossing between Harris and the barely populated island of Scarp was difficult, so Gerhard Zucker tried to send the post by rocket. The end result was a shower of charred paper.

According to a report on STV in 2012, postmen and postwomen are most at risk from dog attacks in the north-east of Scotland, where forty-two were attacked, compared to thirty-six in the Glasgow postcode area.

The Scottish Wildlife Trust owns the Ben Mor Coigach reserve, a wild land north of Ullapool in the north-west Highlands. The 6-mile-long coastal path – not an easy jaunt – is known as the Postie's Path, as it was the route used to take mail to and from the remote township of Achiltibuie. Walking this path makes you realise the heroic lengths postmen used to go in doing their job.

In December 1908 Robert Cunningham, having never once in ten years failed to deliver the post around the lonely South Ayrshire village of Ballantrae, did not let a heavy snowfall deter him. Several days later he was found on the moor, frozen to death, his empty mailsack beneath him. A monument in his memory was erected on the moor in 2008.

A monument at the top of the dramatic hollow known as the Devil's Beef Tub, near Annanhead in Dumfries & Galloway, bears the following dedication: 'Near the head of this burn on 1st Feb., 1831, James McGeorge, guard, and John Goodfellow, driver of the Dumfries to Edinburgh Mail lost their lives in the snow after carrying the bags thus far.'

In the late 1950s Joseph 'Tex' Geddes purchased the island of Soay off the south coast of Skye. When all the other inhabitants requested evacuation from the isolated island, the GPO wanted to cut off all postal and telephone services to Soay. Geddes therefore embarked on a campaign of getting his friends to deluge his one-man island with telegrams and registered packages – some of which just contained stones.

One of the pleasures of going for a walk in the Scottish mountains used to be an early-morning trip to your starting point in a postbus, where for an appropriate fare you could travel in the vehicles delivering mail to remote communities. Sadly postbus services are now endangered species, but there are still a few routes remaining, on the islands of Islay and Luing, the Western Isles, and between Tongue and Lairg in Sutherland (Highland).

For ten years, Keith Knox, a footballer with the Third Division club Clyde FC in Cumbernauld (North Lanarkshire), combined his sporting career with his early-morning job as a postman in Stranraer (Dumfries & Galloway) – a daily round-trip of 200 miles.

TWEED

London, 1832: a cloth merchant opens a letter from William Watson & Sons, of Dangerfield Mills in Hawick. The Borders company, it turns out, wish to bring to the attention of their esteemed customer a new form of cloth made from a weave using two or more differently coloured yarns, known as 'tweel' (a Lowland Scots version of 'twill'). The London merchant, noting Hawick's location close to the River Tweed, mistakes 'tweel' for 'tweed'. And so, with a single misread letter, the distinctive Scottish cloth of tweed is born. Tweed has two principal manufacturing bases: the Borders, and the Western Isles, where Harris Tweed is a registered trademark.

BBC Wales, Cardiff, 2010: Matt Smith, the new Dr Who, appears on screen sporting a tweed jacket. The Western Isles MP Angus MacNeil puckishly comments: 'The endorsement by *Dr Who* shows that Harris Tweed is timeless and can be worn anytime, at any age and in any galaxy.'

10

SPORTS
& GAMES

WALKING

With its variety of scenery and topography, Scotland is ideally suited to the concept of long-distance hiking. One of the most popular routes is the coast-to-coast Southern Upland Way, a 212-mile trek through Dumfries & Galloway and the Scottish Borders. Part of the route is shared with the 94-mile Sir Walter Scott Way, which is arranged around sites associated with Scott's works and life.

The Roman Heritage Way is a T-shaped route, linking the Hadrian's Wall Path across northern England with the line of the Roman military road Dere Street as far as the fort of Trimontium at Melrose in the Scottish Borders.

Another Borders walk with a specific historical interest is the St Cuthbert Way, which runs for 62 miles from Melrose Abbey – where the seventh-century saint began his working life – to the Holy Isle of Lindisfarne on the Northumbrian coast.

Both the islands of Arran and Bute have long-distance coastal paths.

There are around twenty other long-distance routes across the whole of Scotland, from the Cape Wrath Trail in the far north to the Kintyre Way in Argyll. You can find paths named after various aspects of Scottish history and culture: after Rob Roy; conservationist and tree-planter John Muir; the Borders Abbeys; and the Highland cattle-drovers known as Caterans.

Scotland's first end-to-end walk opened in 2012. Starting at Kirk Yetholm on the border with England, the Scottish National Trail runs for 470 miles to Cape Wrath on the north-western tip of Caithness. Walking the entire length takes five to six weeks.

The West Highland Way is Scotland's best-known long-distance footpath. Around 30,000 people complete the 96-mile trek from Milngavie in Glasgow to the Highland town of Fort William each year. If attempting it, bring midge repellent.

GOLF

There are 450 golf courses in Scotland.

At 1,294ft above sea level, the 9th tee at Dufftown Golf Club on Speyside (Moray) is the highest golfing spot in Britain.

'Gowf' has been known in Scotland since the fourteenth century, when it was banned because men preferred playing the game rather than undertaking military training.

'The earliest golf club in the world' is a much-disputed title. Candidates include the Burgess Golfing Society of Edinburgh (probably 1735) and the Honourable Company of Edinburgh Golfers (1744). The Society of St Andrews Golfers followed in 1754.

The St Andrews organisation soon became the Royal & Ancient Golf Club of St Andrews, which is now the rulemaking body for world golf – except for the USA and Mexico.

Scotland markets itself as 'the home of golf'.

The Open, the oldest of the four main annual championships in golf, was first played at Prestwick (South Ayrshire) in 1860. The Open is a UK-wide event and is held at various courses in Scotland for three out of every five years.

What do champion golfers do when they become too old to play professionally? Well, some of them design golf courses. The giants of course architecture are Old Tom Morris, who designed the Old and New Courses in St Andrews, and James Braid of Earlsferry in Fife, who created an incredible 250 courses, including the King's and Queen's Courses at Gleneagles. For golfers, St Andrews (Fife) and Gleneagles (Perth & Kinross) are heavenly twins.

Braid's final design, at Stranraer in Dumfries & Galloway, was completed in 1950; he died, aged 80, shortly afterwards. Like many touched with genius, he was a tad eccentric, never using a tape measure, and working out distances by simply using the length of his stride. Braid had a fear of flying and got seasick on the calmest ocean. As a result the greatest golf course designer of his generation never took up the lucrative offers waiting for him in America.

Although the Ryder Cup, which is played every two years between Europe and America, had its official birth in Massachusetts in 1927, the contest's origins go back to 1921, when an American team travelled on the Cunard liner RMS *Aquitania* to play the Glasgow Herald Thousand Guineas Tournament on James Braid's new course at Gleneagles. This was the first-ever international golf match – and the ten-man American team included four native Scots who had gone to seek their fortune across the Atlantic. The score? Great Britain & Ireland 9, the United States of America 3.

The opening scenes of the Oscar-winning 1981 film *Chariots of Fire*, set to Vangelis' uplifting electronic soundtrack, shows athletes training for the 1924 Olympics running in slow motion across the West Sands at St Andrews. In the foreground, the stars, Ian Charleson and Ben Cross; in the background, the other runners, most of whom were the town's golf caddies.

SAILING

For a truly spectacular day out, head for Crinan in Argyll, where each July the second leg of the Tobermory Yacht Race sees around 200 yachts racing for the narrow channel. Be warned, however, that the timing of the race is governed by the turning of the tide, so it can start as early as 4 a.m.

SWIMMING

In 1947 the marathon swimmer Thomas Blower – who had already swum the English Channel – became the first person to swim from Northern Ireland to Scotland. The 22-mile crossing from Donaghadee in

County Down to Portpatrick in Wigtownshire (Dumfries & Galloway) took fifteen hours and thirty-one minutes. Blower followed the Short Sea Route, the shortest port-to-port Ireland-Scotland crossing, on which ships ran for 200 years from 1662 until the route was replaced by the boats operating between Larne and Stranraer, which had a better harbour than Portpatrick.

HORSE RACING

In the nineteenth century a butler always bet on the same horse – which won fifty-one out of sixty-four races, including the Ascot Gold Cup. Retiring on his winnings, the gambler bought an inn in Dumfries & Galloway and named it after the horse – Beeswing. A village of the same name has since grown up on the Dumfries to Dalbeattie road.

HIGHLAND GAMES

Highland Games are traditional: which is to say, they were largely invented during the Victorian era.

Trials of strength and speed were a known part of Highland culture from medieval times, although these were rarely formally organised. All such activities were banned after the Jacobite Rebellion of 1745 by the subsequent Act of Proscription, which forbade clansmen meeting in groups, as well as the playing of bagpipes. When the Act was repealed in 1782, 'gatherings' and sporting events started to be reinstituted.

The first recorded, formal, modern-style Highland Games took place at Braemar in Aberdeenshire in 1832. Twelve years later Queen Victoria attended a Highland Games, and lent the royal seal of approval to this activity which was, like so many things in Scotland at the time, both old and revived, and new and invented.

Braemar is close to Balmoral Castle; members of the Royal Family are therefore often seen attending the games at Braemar.

In a typical summer there will be around forty Highland Games across the country, from Durness on the far north coast to North Berwick in East Lothian (which is of course nowhere near the Highlands).

In terms of participants, the Cowal Highland Gathering is the largest Highland Games in the world. The event at Dunoon (Argyll & Bute) regularly attracts 3,500 entrants, including dancers, pipers and drum majors.

The massed pipe bands and Highland dancing aside, most people are interested in the 'heavies': the stone putt, the hammer throw, the weight throw and – especially – the caber toss.

The caber is a long – very long – piece of wood. It may be a larch tree denuded of branches, or even a telegraph pole. Although weights and lengths vary, a typical caber will tip the scales at 175lbs and be slightly less than 20ft tall. The competitor has to hold it vertically in his hands, run forward, and then toss it up so that it turns end-over-end, with – hopefully – the top end landing on the ground and balancing there before falling horizontally.

No Highland Games is complete without a tug-o'-war, a favourite with rugby teams and military units. All together now: Heave!

A curious recent addition to the games is the sheaf toss, where a sheaf of straw has to be hoisted over a raised bar – using a pitchfork.

FISHING

The 'Royal Four Towns Fishing Order Confirmation Act 1965' confirmed a set of special privileges conferred by Robert the Bruce in the fourteenth century on four small villages in Dumfries & Galloway. The residents of Hightae, Greenhill, Smallholm and Heck have the right to fish for free on a 3½-mile stretch of the River Annan, and this right is included in the estate agent description of all properties for sale in the area.

By law, there is no salmon fishing in Scottish rivers on a Sunday. Other species, such as brown trout, can be caught on any day of the week.

SHINTY

It's not hockey, but it is played with a wooden stick (caman) and a ball. It's not ice hockey, although it probably inspired it. It's not Irish hurling, although the two sports are sufficiently similar that Ireland can play Scotland using composite rules. It's shinty, a distinctively Scottish Highland game – and very exciting, fast and physical it is too.

What makes shinty different is that the ball can be played in the air – and so a skilled player can run with the ball bouncing off the horizontal stick – 'keepy-uppy'.

The current shinty pitch is between 140 and 170 yards long. When the game was first regulated in the late nineteenth century, the pitch was twice that length. Victorian teams were originally sixteen strong; that number has now been reduced to twelve. Before the game was formalised, rural shinty matches at Hogmanay (New Year) could involve dozens, if not hundreds, of participants.

The ancestor sport of both shinty and Irish hurling was known to have been played in Ireland about 2,000 years ago, when it was regarded as suitable training for warriors. Shinty travelled from Ireland with the Scottish colonists, and so has probably been played on the west coast of Scotland since around the fifth century AD.

The rules of the modern sport were developed between 1887 and 1893.

Shinty or its variants have been known by many names – hailes, knotty, cammon, cammock, cluich-bhall and others. The modern Gaelic names are camanachd and iomain.

Shinty is played at both league and cup level. The 'big two' teams have traditionally been Kingussie and their neighbour-rivals Newtonmore (both in Badenoch, Highland). Other major teams are found at Inverness, Drumnadrochit, Balmacara, Spean Bridge and Fort William in the Highlands, and at Oban, Inveraray and Tighnabruaich in Argyll.

The most consistently successful league team ever known in shinty is Kingussie Camanachd, who were the league champions for the twenty consecutive years up to 2005. Kingussie have also won the Camanachd Cup 22 times, although Newtonmore hold the cup record, with 28 wins.

Scottish universities have a long tradition of fielding shinty teams – the Edinburgh University Shinty Club, for example, was founded as early as 1891. Other university teams include Aberdeen, Dundee, Glasgow, Robert Gordon (in Aberdeen), St Andrews and Strathclyde (in Glasgow). The British Armed Forces also field a team, which has gone through several name changes to be currently known as SCOTS Camanachd.

Shinty travelled with Highland emigrants, and in the nineteenth century could be found in Lowland Scotland, London, the industrial north of England, and North America. It is currently enjoying a revival in several of these locations.

TENNIS

In 1437 a group of nobles burst into the apartments of King James I in Perth, intent on murder. James attempted to escape down a sewer –

but on his own orders it had just been blocked up because he kept losing his tennis balls down the drain. He did not live to appreciate the irony.

When Dunblane's Andy Murray won the Men's Singles Championship at Wimbledon in 2013, he was the first British person to do so for seventy-seven years. The only other Scot ever to triumph at Wimbledon, meanwhile, was Edinburgh's Harold Mahony in 1896, when tennis players still wore long trousers and a shirt and tie.

Murray was one of the survivors of the Dunblane Massacre in 1996, when a gunman killed eighteen people, including sixteen primary school children.

BASEBALL

Not perhaps a game usually associated with Scotland, there are several teams currently playing in Glasgow and Edinburgh, the game apparently having been introduced by US airmen stationed over here in the 1960s.

A number of players in the American major leagues were born in Scotland. The earliest was Jim McCormick of Glasgow, who debuted with the Indianapolis Browns in 1878.

Perhaps the most renowned baseball player of Scottish origin is Bobby Thomson, originally from Glasgow, who scored the winning home run for the New York Giants in the 1951 World Series, an event famously described at the time as 'the shot heard around the world' – a reference to the large number of American servicemen who were tuning in from overseas.

In October 1942 Hampden Park Stadium in Glasgow hosted an American Games Day. Before a crowd of almost 30,000 spectators, including actor Edward G. Robinson, US servicemen en route to the war in North Africa played baseball (the Yankees *v.* the Cardinals) and American football (the Chicago Bears *v.* the Green Bay Packers). The American military was still racially segregated, so black servicemen could not participate in these events. Instead, two all-black teams, the 'Homestead Greys' and the 'Harlem Eagles', competed in a game of softball.

CHESS

In 1831 one of the oldest chess sets in Europe spilled out of a sandbank at Uig on Lewis in the Western Isles. Carved from walrus ivory and whale teeth, the seventy-eight pieces (representing parts of five sets) are Scandinavian in origin and probably date from around 1150. With their bulging eyes, grotesque or comic expressions, and Viking 'berserker' behaviours such as shield-biting, the pieces are irresistibly fascinating to modern eyes. Sixty-seven are on display in London's British Museum, while the remaining eleven form one of the most popular exhibits at the Museum of Scotland in Edinburgh.

FOOTBALL

Football had its own Act of Parliament in medieval Scotland. The Football Act of 1424, passed into law by King James I, made the playing of football illegal, with malefactors having to pay a fine of 4*d*.

The Act was not officially taken off the Statute books until 1906.

'The fut ball' was again expressly banned in several subsequent laws. Mostly this was because it interfered with wappenschaws or 'weapon shows', where the men of the district were compelled to gather for weapons training. Partly, however, football was unpopular with the authorities because it was so violent. Basically, the game involved a ball – and hardly any rules. Broken bones were common. Some players could be crippled for life.

The first football club in Scotland was formed in 1867, when Queen's Park in Glasgow followed the rules of Association Football set out for the first time four years previously.

In the early days there were fewer players and fewer clubs, and in 1870, when a challenge was issued for a Scotland–England match in London, very few players came forward (the Scotland team ended up being mostly Scots living in England).

By the late 1880s football was the most popular sport in Glasgow and the industrial Lowlands.

The Scottish Football League began in 1890. The English Football League had been founded two years earlier – set up by a Scotsman, William MacGregor, originally from Braco in Perth & Kinross.

The 1890/91 League season ended with two joint winners – the Glasgow-based Rangers FC, and Dumbarton FC.

The Scottish Professional Football League is currently organised into the Scottish Premier League, and the First, Second and Third Divisions, giving a total of forty-two clubs. Below them are the thirty clubs of the Highland League and the Lowland League, and then the hundreds of clubs in non-professional football.

Some local clubs have names that clearly reflect their specific origins: Inverurie Loco Works, Forres Mechanics, Civil Service Strollers, Burntisland Shipyard, and Easthouses Lily Miners Welfare.

It is estimated that on any given Saturday, 34 per cent of Scottish males will watch or listen to a football match, whether as a spectator or as part of a radio or television audience.

Berwick Rangers FC play in the Scottish Third Division. They are based in England.

THE BA' GAME

An insight into the roughhouse nature of medieval football can be gained by looking at the 'mob' ball games that have survived or been revived – the ba' games.

Historically, ba' games are known to have taken place in Glasgow, Scone (Perth & Kinross), and Duns and Roxburgh (both in the Scottish Borders). The 'rules' in each case were different, but largely revolved around sizeable disorderly groups pushing and shoving in the streets of the town and trying to get the ba' or ball to a specific point.

Two places where ba' games can still be seen are Jedburgh in the Scottish Borders and, at the other end of Scotland, Kirkwall in the Orkney Islands. Although the former uses several balls and the latter just one, both have teams designated as 'Uppies' or 'Downies', depending on which part of the town you or family hail from.

As most of the participants rarely know where the ba' is at any given moment, it can be 'smuggled' out in clothing, or one player can pretend to have the ba', while the real ba' is moving secretly towards its goal. Lanes, alleys, shop doorways and even roofs can be used, especially in the larger and more intense Kirkwall Ba'.

On one infamous occasion the Kirkwall players invaded the local police station.

The first Jedburgh or Jephart Ba' game used not a leather ball but – so the story goes – an Englishman's head. The ribbons attached to the ba' supposedly represent the hair of said individual. The thing about this story is that it may be a load of nonsense – or it may be true.

Serious injuries are rare these days – the people most at risk are the spectators, who may be caught by a sudden unexpected mass shove in a previously immobile huddle.

The Kirkwall Ba' Games always takes place on Christmas Day and New Year's Day – unless they fall on a Sunday, it which case each game is postponed for a day. The Jedburgh Ba' timetable is more peculiar, being the first Thursday after Shrove Tuesday in early February – but it also be the week after, depending on the date of the new moon.

The average Ba' Game in Kirkwall lasts five hours. It has been known to take longer than eight hours.

BIBLIOGRAPHY

Anderson, Alan Orr (ed.), *Early Sources of Scottish History AD 500–1286* (Paul Watkins: Stanford, 1990)

Arnold, H.R., *Atlas of Mammals in Britain* (HMSO: London, 1993)

Automobile Association, *Secret Britain* (Automobile Association: Basingstoke, 1986)

Baptie, B., *UK Earthquake Monitoring 2005/2006* (British Geological Survey Commissioned Report, OR/07/010: 2007)

Barrett, Michael, *A Calendar of Scottish Saints* (The Abbey Press: Fort Augustus, 1919)

Barthrop, Michael, *The Jacobite Rebellions* (Osprey Publishing: Oxford, 1982)

Baxter, J.M., et al (eds), *Scotland's Marine Atlas: Information for the National Marine Plan* (Marine Scotland: Edinburgh, 2011)

Bruce, David, *Scotland: The Movie* (Polygon: Edinburgh, 1996)

Bryden, D.M., et al, *Assessing the Economic Impacts of Nature Based Tourism in Scotland* (Scottish Natural Heritage: Inverness, 2010)

Buczacki, Stefan, *Fauna Britannica* (Hamlyn: London, 2002)

Burne, A. H., *The Agincourt War: A Military History of the Latter Part of the Hundred Years War from 1369 to 1453* (Folio Society: London, 2005 [1956])

Business and Enterprise Statistics, *Businesses in Scotland 2012* (Scottish Government: Glasgow, 2012)

Cameron, Alexander, *The History and Traditions of the Isle of Skye* (E. Forsyth: Inverness, 1871)

Campbell, James, *Invisible Country: A Journey through Scotland* (Weidenfeld and Nicolson: London, 1984)

Casely, Gordon, 'Those magnificent Scots and their flying machines', *The Leopard* (December, 2003)

Chambers, Robert, *The Domestic Annals of Scotland* (W & R Chambers: Edinburgh and London, 1858)

Coldham, Peter Wilson, *Emigrants in Chains: A Social History of Forced Emigration to the Americas of Felons, Destitute Children, Political and Religious Non-Conformists, Vagabonds, Beggars and Other Undesirables, 1607–1776* (Genealogical Publishing Company: Baltimore, 1994)

Coren, Stanley, *The Intelligence of Dogs*, (Bantam Books: New York, 1994)

Cowan, Ian B., *The Scottish Covenanters, 1660–1688* (Victor Gollancz: London, 1976)

Curley, Thomas M., *Samuel Johnson, the Ossian Fraud, and the Celtic Revival in Great Britain and Ireland* (Cambridge University Press: Cambridge, 2009)

Cuthbertson, D.C., *Highlands, Highways and Heroes: or, Wandering in the Westlands* (Robert Grant and Son: Edinburgh, 1931)

Davison, Charles, *A History of British Earthquakes* (Cambridge University Press: Cambridge, 1924)

Donaldson, Gordon, *Scotland from James V to James VII* (Oliver & Boyd: Edinburgh & London, 1965)

Douglas, David, *Early Travellers in Scotland* (James Maclehose & Sons: Glasgow, 1891)

Driscoll, Stephen, *Alba: The Gaelic Kingdom of Scotland AD 800–1124* (Birlinn: Edinburgh, 2002)

Furgol, Edward M., 'The Scottish itinerary of Mary Queen of Scots, 1542–8 and 1561–8', *Proceedings of the Society of Antiquaries of Scotland*, Vol. 117 (1987)

Galloway, D.D. (ed.), *Bulletin of British Earthquakes 2011* (British Geological Survey Internal Report, OR/12/041: Nottingham, 2012)

Gordon, Seton, *Highways and Byways in the Central Highlands* (Birlinn: Edinburgh, 1995 [1935])

Gordon-Cumming, C.F., *In The Hebrides* (Chatto and Windus: London, 1883)

Groome, Frances H. (ed.), *Ordnance Gazetteer of Scotland: A Survey of Scottish Topography, Statistical, Biographical and Historical* (Grange Publishing Works: Edinburgh, 1882-1885)

Haswell-Smith, Hamish, *The Scottish Islands* (Canongate: Edinburgh, 1996)

Historic Scotland, *Spotlight on Scotland's Cinemas* (Historic Scotland: Edinburgh, 2009)

Hodge, Ed, *Jewel In The Glen: Gleneagles, Golf and The Ryder Cup* (Arena Sport/Birlinn: Edinburgh, 2013)

Holder, Geoff, *The Guide to Mysterious Perthshire* (Tempus: Stroud, 2006)

Holder, Geoff, *The Guide to Mysterious Loch Ness and the Inverness Area* (Tempus: Stroud, 2007)

Holder, Geoff, *The Guide to Mysterious Stirlingshire* (The History Press: Stroud, 2008)

Holder, Geoff, *The Guide to Mysterious Aberdeenshire* (The History Press: Stroud, 2009)

Holder, Geoff, *The Guide to Mysterious Skye and Lochalsh* (The History Press: Stroud, 2010)

Hutchinson, R., *Camanachd: The Story of Shinty* (Mainstream Publishing: Edinburgh, 1989)

Hutton, Guthrie, *Lanarkshire's Mining Legacy* (Stenlake Publishing: Catrine, 1997)

Irving, Gordon, *The Devil on Wheels* (Alloway Publishing: Darvel, 1986)

Jackson, Anthony, *The Pictish Trail: A Traveller's Guide to the Old Pictish Kingdoms* (The Orkney Press: Kirkwall, 1989)

Keay, John, and Julia Keay (eds), *Collins Encyclopaedia of Scotland* (HarperCollins: London, 1994)

Keith, Alexander, *A Thousand Years of Aberdeen* (Aberdeen University Press: Aberdeen, 1972)

Laing, Lloyd, and Jenny Laing, *The Picts and the Scots* (Sutton: Stroud, 1998)

Lees, J. Cameron, *A History of the County of Inverness* (Blackwood: Edinburgh, 1897)

McClure, David, *Tolls and Tacksmen* (Ayrshire Monographs No.13, AANHS: Ayr, 1994)

McClure, David, (ed.), *Ayrshire in the Age of Improvement* (Ayrshire Monographs No. 27, AANHS: Ayr, 2002)

Mackenzie, Alexander, *The History of the Highland Clearances* (A. & W. Mackenzie: Inverness, 1883)

McKerracher, Mairead, *The Jacobite Dictionary* (Neil Wilson Publishing: Glasgow, 2007)

McNeish, Cameron, *The Munros: Scotland's Highest Mountains* (Lomond Books: Broxburn, 1998)

Mason, Roger (ed.), *Scotland and England, 1286–1815* (John Donald: Edinburgh, 1987)

Millar, W.J., *The Clyde: From Its Source to The Sea* (Blackie: London, 1888)

Moffat, Alistair, and Dr Jim Wilson, *The Scots: A Genetic Journey* (Birlinn: Edinburgh, 2011)

Newton, Michael, *A Handbook of the Scottish Gaelic World* (Four Courts Press: Dublin, 2000)

Paine, Robin and Roger Syms, *On a Cushion of Air* (Robin Paine & Roger Syms/Writersworld: Woodstock, 2012)

Palmer, Geoff, *The Enlightenment Abolished: Citizens of Britishness* (Henry Publishing: Penicuik, 2007)

Platt, Richard, *Smuggling in the British Isles: A History* (The History Press: Stroud, 2011)

If you enjoyed this book, you may also be interested in…

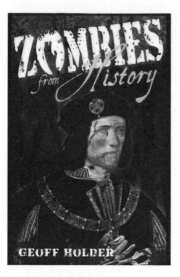

Zombies from History
GEOFF HOLDER

Are you worried about the zombie apocalypse? Well, fret no more! With full zombie-hunting details – including the locations of tombs, weaknesses and a carefully calculated difficulty rating, this book is the ultimate guide to some of history's most famous names, and what to do if they try to eat your face.

978 0 7524 9964 2

The Little Book of Hogmanay
BOB PEGG

The Little Book of Hogmanay is a feast of information exploring the history, folklore, customs, food, drink and celebrations of Hogmanay, from its roots to its present. Whether you need a user's guide or an anthology of entertainment, this book will tell you all you ever wanted to know about Scotland's most widely, and wildly, celebrated festival.

978 0 7524 8964 3

Visit our website and discover thousands of other History Press books.

www.thehistorypress.co.uk

The History Press